The Return

Elbert D. Charpie

Prewrathministries.org

The Return

How to Understand the Scriptures

"IS THERE A WAY TO UNDERSTAND END-TIME PROPHECY WHERE ALL THE PIECES JUST FALL INTO PLACE NATURALLY?"

Pentastic
PUBLISHING

PREWRATH MINISTRIES
WHAT THE SCRIPTURES SAYS ABOUT THE END OF TIME

Contact Elbert Charpie
www.prewrathministries.org

Published in York, SC by Pentastic Publishing

All scripture quotations, unless otherwise indicated, are taken from the Holy Bible, King James Version, Cambridge, 1769 (public domain).

Scripture quotations marked (NIV) are taken from the Holy Bible, New International Version®, NIV®. Copyright © 1973, 1978, 1984, 2011 by Biblica, Inc.™ Used by permission of Zondervan. All rights reserved worldwide. www.zondervan.com The "NIV" and "New International Version" are trademarks registered in the United States Patent and Trademark Office by Biblica, Inc.™

Cover photos public domain.
Cover design help: Robert Kell

Library of Congress Cataloging-in-Publication Data
Charpie, Elbert,
    The return of Christ: how to understand the scriptures / Elbert Charpie
        p. cm
    ISBN 978-0-9882063-1-1 (pbk.)
1.   End of the world. 2. Rapture (Christian eschatology) 3. Prophecy-
Christianity. I. Title.
Manufactured in the United States of America

LU11012014

Dedicated to my wife, Vickie
and my children:
Paul & Amy
Rachel
Daniel
and my granddaughter
Avalyn
and in memory of her sister
Laelyn

Table of Contents

Table of Figures

Acknowledgments

Thomas Dismukes: I would have never thought this possible without you. You continue to make the unbelievable believable!

Pam Tucker: She is the wife of my best friend and one of the smartest ladies I have ever met. I could not have done this without your excellent eye for editing.

Randy Von Kanel for pointing me in the right direction.

Grace Baptist Church in Johnson City, Tennessee: You listened as I taught something completely different, and you didn't run me off!

First Baptist Church Citronelle, Alabama: You continue to encourage and support me as your pastor. Your confidence and patience in my teaching made this possible.

Special thanks to Charles Cooper, who put up with a thousand questions, as I tried to work out my theology.

Special thanks to Robert Van Kampen for writing the following books: *The Sign*, *The Rapture Question Answered*, and Marvin Rosenthal for: *The PreWrath Rapture of the Church*. Your works helped me understand what the scriptures really do teach.

Introduction
Why Is It So Confusing?

In seminary, I remember discussions among students, who were deep in opinions and shallow in knowledge, and sooner or later the topic would come up regarding the second coming of Christ. Various doctrines would be dressed up in labels making them sound more profound such as "amillennial," "pre-tribulational," and "preterist," but the truth was most of these students were spouting the teachings they had heard, including myself. We had not searched the scriptures to find what the Bible actually does teach. Reading the scriptures and teaching the specifics of Christ's return, I found myself more confused because the descriptions of the events and the flow of the narrative did not seem to match all the sermons and teachings I had heard most of my life. I had to attempt to satisfy myself with the following conclusion: the topic of Christ's return was either too complicated, or the scriptures do not give us enough information in order to fully grasp the subject.

As a result, many of the students would profess to be "pan-millennialists." These students were those who subscribed to the non-scriptural conclusion it really did not matter how God would plan for Christ's return because it would all "pan-out" in the end. Although, the doctrine of the return of Christ is not a crucial issue having a bearing on our salvation, the multitude of scripture dealing with the return of Christ insists God intends for His people to know about how Christ will return, and to live expecting His return. In addition, the scripture contains multiple warnings to watch and be ready.

Another element contributing to the questions surrounding Christ's return is the prevalence of so many packaged ideas about the second coming. Doctrinal labels have been invented to wrap these packages to make them more attractive and readily accepted. Many people adhere strongly to these labels

11

without really knowing what they mean. A professor will proclaim to his students that he is amillennial, and so the students decide they must also be amillennial because of the great respect they have for their mentor. These students have a commitment to a doctrine which they do not have the intellectual integrity to defend.

As a pastor when one of my church members suggested I should preach on the second coming of Christ; I felt the fear of attempting to teach a subject of which I also struggled to understand. I believed what I had always been taught, but when I would study the scriptures, I would end up with more questions than answers. I had a label, but I could not defend it in the scriptures. I believe many people approach the topic of the return of Christ with the same intimidation. I would often preach and teach about Christ's return in general; however, never go into specifics.

A few years later, I had a friend refer me to a book which took an unconventional approach to the coming of Christ which had a strong scriptural foundation for its premise. Because I was so indoctrinated in what I had been taught all my life, I argued with my friend over the book. I discovered I had little scriptural basis for my position. I spent time digging through the scriptures and was surprised to make two discoveries: I learned that my long-held view of the second coming was totally unscriptural. Consequently, even more surprising, I found understanding what the scriptures truly teach about Christ's return was not difficult when I removed all of the assumptions and presuppositions I had used like a pair of glasses through which to interpret the scriptures.

I poured through the few books I could find explaining the second coming of Christ from this scriptural approach; I was disappointed in the perspective within the books. These books had the authority of sound biblical evidence which should have been all that was required, but I found these authors took a defensive stand against the accepted popular views of Christ's coming to the point of being antagonistic. This defensive posture was totally unnecessary, and I decided to develop my own study concerning the return of Christ which would stand totally on the merit of biblical study.

I began teaching this study and was amazed at the response. People would come to me and say, "Finally the scriptural prophecies really made sense." A few people shared my own conflict of recognizing the scriptural evidence; but yet resisting the adoption of this new approach because it meant a change in theology which I had previously taught for years. In addition, popular theology is much more attractive to our natural desires than what the scriptures actually teach, but does it not hold true of most biblical principles? So, the basis of this book is the attempt to put my study in printed form without the emotional bias I found in other authors. Step by step, I plan to examine popular theology against the scriptures and uncover the biblical blueprint for Christ's return.

I have described this approach to prophecy as "New." However, the more I studied, the more I discovered what I had been taught all my life was actually a new interpretation. It had only been taught since the turn of the 20th century. Although, the approach I came to accept was packaged as "New," with a new label; the interpretation contained in this new approach could be found in the teachings of the early church fathers[1], as well as the scriptures themselves.

One last note, I have used the King James Version of the Bible throughout this study. However, where the meaning of the text is not as clear, I have chosen to use the New International Version of the Bible. I am aware there are more accurate and scholarly translations available, but I find the NIV more readable and understandable, and my purpose is for the reader to understand the scripture.

---

[1] Examples of the teachings of early church fathers that support this new approach can be found in the Appendix.

Chapter 1
What It Could Look Like

Before moving into the technical outline of scriptural prophecy, it may be helpful for the reader to get an idea of how scriptural prophecy will unfold. Therefore, chapter one will attempt to provide a narrative of how the return of Christ could happen based on the details contained in the subsequent chapters. Liberty will be taken to imagine how some of the events could take place in order to illustrate what will happen.

The Seventieth Week of Daniel

At some point the Antichrist will emerge on the scene and will be instrumental in fashioning a covenant between Israel and many other nations. In Daniel 9:27, it states he will "confirm" the covenant. Whether this indicates he establishes the covenant or ratifies a proposed covenant; the covenant will inaugurate the beginning of the 70th Week of Daniel. The Jewish people will accept this covenant as the answer for a final peace. They will trust in the Antichrist.

In Matthew 24, Jesus was instructing His followers, and He gave them the signal for which they should be watching.

> **Matt 24:15** (NIV) "So when you see standing in the holy place `the abomination that causes desolation,' spoken of through the prophet Daniel -- let the reader understand..."

Jesus told His followers to be watching for the Abomination of Desolation and not the signing of the covenant. Therefore, it is possible the covenant may not be a publicized or notable event which would be obvious to God's people. Because Jesus stated to watch for the Abomination of Desolation, the possibility exists that God's people may not realize the 70th Week of Daniel has started until the Abomination of Desolation. By that time, 3 ½ years of the 70th Week will have already passed. During the first half of the 70th Week of Daniel, the Antichrist will be solidifying his power. As there have been, there will be wars and rumors of wars, earthquakes and famine. Toward the middle of the 70th Week, the Antichrist will set his sights on Jerusalem.

> **Matthew 24:16** Then let them which be in Judaea flee into the mountains:

We are told the Antichrist will set himself up in God's temple and claim to be God. At this point, he will demand that the entire world worship him. Many religions in the world are looking for a deliverer. Christians are looking for the return of Christ. Jews are awaiting the Messiah. Islam is anxious for the return of the 12th Imam. It is possible the Antichrist could claim to embody all of these in order to consolidate the religions of the world.

> **2 Thessalonians 2:3** Let no man deceive you by any means: for that day shall not come, except there come a falling away first, and that **man of sin be revealed**, the son of perdition; 4 Who opposeth and exalteth himself above all that is called God, or that is worshipped; so that **he as God** sitteth in the temple of God, **shewing himself that he is God** (emphasis added).

When the Antichrist reveals himself at the Abomination of Desolation, the Jewish people will immediately recognize their error. They will reject the Antichrist and flee from Jerusalem and the surrounding areas. A great number will escape to Edom where they will be protected by God. Others will go into hiding wherever they can.

16

In the city of Jerusalem, two men appear on the temple mount, and they begin to preach to the world that the judgment of God is coming. Furious guards and by passers attempt to attack these two witnesses and fire comes from their mouths and destroys those who would seek to harm them. On their command plagues and droughts begin to happen all over the world. Every once in a while these men will appear on newscasts as they destroy attackers, and they are portrayed as terrorists.

At the rejection of the Jewish people the Antichrist immediately begins a campaign of persecution against the Jews, but he has little success. His army pursues them into the wilderness, but the battalion is never heard from again. Therefore, he turns his attention to the Christians; those who worship Jesus Christ. The Antichrist begins a systematic campaign of persecuting the followers of Jesus. Many begin to fall away from the faith and many are martyred.

> **Matt 24:9** Then shall they deliver you up to be afflicted, and shall kill you: and ye shall be hated of all nations for my name's sake. 10 And then shall many be offended, and shall betray one another, and shall hate one another.

The Rapture

Sometime during the second half of the 70th Week of Daniel, after the persecution of Christians has occurred, the world is astounded as the sun turns black and the moon turns dark red. The stars appear to fall from the sky as the sky appears to be rolled back like a scroll. The sign of the Son of Man, possibly the cross, appears in the heavens and the entire earth witnesses Jesus Christ coming on the clouds in power and great glory. There is a loud trumpet call as Jesus sends His angels to gather His people from one end of the earth to the other. Graves open up as the dead in Christ are resurrected. All God's people are caught up to meet the Lord Jesus in the air, and the entire world bears witness.

On earth, all those who have rejected Jesus Christ are terrified. They are not able to stand before the glorious presence of the Lamb of God. They try to hide from Him, and there is a stark recognition by all people on the earth; the God of this universe is Jesus Christ. They realize judgment day has come. Some repent; however, most still refuse to honor Jesus as Lord.

The Antichrist tries to explain what has happened; the Lord God sends a strong delusion, so the world believes his lie.

> **2 Thessalonians 2:9** (NIV) The coming of the lawless one will be in accordance with the work of Satan displayed in all kinds of counterfeit miracles, signs and wonders, 10 and in every sort of evil that deceives those who are perishing. **They perish because they refused to love the truth and so be saved**. 11 For this reason **God sends them a powerful delusion so that they will believe the lie** 12 and so that all will be condemned who have not believed the truth but have delighted in wickedness (emphasis added).

As the world settles down trusting the wisdom of the Antichrist, in the background can be heard the voices of the two witnesses declaring Christ has come.

The Trumpet Judgments

The first angel sounds his trumpet. After a time, things begin to get back to normal. The Antichrist consoles the world, and they trust in Him. Then, one morning as the world begins their day, huge storm clouds form as lightning ignites hailstones which fall from the sky, and the rain that is mixed in with the hail becomes blood and falls upon the entire earth. One third of the entire earth is burned up along with one-third of all trees and there is no grass left.

People are reminded of the wrath of God, and the two witnesses continue to preach the judgment of God.

The second angel sounds his trumpet. The world is shocked as news reports from around the globe show footage of a huge volcano which appears in the middle of the Pacific Ocean. It is larger than any mountain on earth and spews lava and toxic debris into the ocean. The entire Pacific Ocean is turned to blood and all the creatures of the sea die and begin to wash up on the shores of the world. The smell of decay permeates the air everywhere in the world. The ocean has turned to blood and enormous amounts of dead sea creatures float on top of the sea stranding ships. The news reports estimate the destruction of the Pacific Ocean amounts to one-third of all the seas on the earth.

The third angel sounds his trumpet. One evening the news begins to report space agencies are tracking an object headed toward earth. Some say it is a meteor, others call it a comet. There are fanatical analysts that predict a collision could mean the end of all life on earth. As the flaming object enters the earth's atmosphere it breaks up into three parts. The news reports begin to announce that God has protected us; we are saved since the comet has broken up. One piece ends up hitting the Great Lakes. One piece hits Lake Victoria in Africa, and the last piece falls into Lake Baikal in Russia. The news commentators jest at how the comet must have been attracted to water, and mention the irony that each piece fell into some of the largest bodies of fresh water on earth. Within a week frantic reports surface that people are dying from drinking contaminated water. It began in America, Africa and Russia. The flow of the water tables has caused the contamination to spread and some estimate that as much as one-third of the fresh water on earth may be affected. News reports still appear about the lunatic preachers in Jerusalem declaring the judgment of God.

The fourth angel sounds his trumpet. After the contamination of fresh water, the governments of the world led by the Antichrist decide to launch satellites into orbit to help provide a better warning system should any kind of meteor approach the earth again. As the attention of the world is drawn to space, a huge solar flare is detected and the sun goes dark. Panic breaks out over the entire world. Police forces are dispatched and martial law is enacted throughout the world to contain the panic. However, after four hours the sun comes back out, and people begin to regain their composure. No one can explain exactly what has happened. There are only about eight hours of daylight from about seven in the morning until three in the afternoon. It is completely dark from three in the afternoon until about midnight when the stars begin to come out. The news media becomes attracted to the two preachers in Jerusalem as they begin to predict greater judgments to come. Their voices can be heard in the background saying, "Woe to the inhabitants of the earth for the three trumpets which are about to sound." People adjusted rather quickly to the one-third less daylight.

The fifth angel sounds his trumpet. It seems quite some time has passed since any global catastrophe has fallen. It is amazing how complacent people can become in such a short time. People were just beginning to get accustomed to the lack of troubling events when NASA alerts began sounding. Once again an object of celestial origin was headed toward the earth. It appeared, once again, to be a star or a comet. Tensions began to rise as global alerts were put into place. The world was glued to the news reports tracking the unknown object as it raced toward the earth.

Astronomers continue to update their projections as the trajectory of this falling star begins to become more apparent. The path of the object narrows from a large cone to a pinpoint path, and the target is determined to be Antarctica. A worldwide sigh of relief is felt as scientists and analysts present their findings showing minimal effect from the impact. If it had not been for the newscasts, no one would have even known the collision took place. It seemed as though a catastrophe had been averted. For the next several days, the news contained reports of scientists exploring the site of impact. The witnesses in Jerusalem proclaimed, "Abaddon is coming!"

Again, news reports were astir as excited scientists began reporting from the meteor site in Antarctica. Seismic activity had been detected and rumors of extraterrestrial activity begin to abound. Once again, the attention of the world became focused to the news with wild expectations of first contact with real-life aliens. Star Trek parties began to crop up all over the world in expectation of the new discovery. The seismic activity increases exponentially as the hours pass, and the world watches in expectation. Suddenly, the ground lurched and from the impact site smoke began to rise. The workers at the impact site began an emergency evacuation when the ground exploded and volcanic smoke and ash began to rise into the atmosphere. A stunned world watched in amazement. Within hours the entire southern hemisphere became clouded with smoke and ash. As the smoke thickened, a buzzing sound as if a thousand helicopters were flying through the smoke could be heard. The news reports began screaming that the aliens were hostile. Incredible creatures rose from the abyss at the impact site. They were a combination of insect and animal. They flew with a roaring sound and a shrill screech as they attacked every human being within reach. The creatures would bite and claw, but their greatest danger was the sting in their tails. Those who were stung suffered more than was thought humanly possible. Victims would cry out for someone to kill them. Some would attempt suicide; however, the amazing side effect of the venom of these creatures was an incredible ability to heal. In searing pain, people would jump off buildings and break their necks, but before death could come their injuries would heal. However, the pain did not stop. By the end of the week, the entire world was under the attack of these hideous creatures. The only people who seemed immune were the Jewish people and some who were labelled religious fanatics. For five months the torment continued. Then, suddenly, without explanation it stopped.

The world reeled from the attack of the alien creatures. Even after the creatures had disappeared for some time, people still hid in terror frozen by fear for what they had suffered through the past five months. The entire earth was deathly quiet like walking through a ghost town. People who had to go out went as quickly and quietly as possible. It seemed the earth itself waited for what would come next.

The sixth angel sounds his trumpet. In order to bring some reason back into the world, a reporter from a major news station decided to put together a story on the two preachers on the temple mount in Jerusalem. After all, they are the heralds of the judgment and gloom that had seemed to fall upon the world. The reporter sets himself up a good distance from the two troublemakers so they can be seen in the newscast at a great distance in the background. The reporter begins his telecast, "Hello, I am live at the temple mount in Jerusalem covering the two terrorists who have continued to plague our world claiming we are under the judgment of God. As the world has encountered terrible catastrophes in the past few months, it is necessary to point out the source of much of our trouble." As people around the world watched the newscast, they saw the television screen shake as it displayed the terrified look on the newscaster's face when he turned and saw the two witnesses standing immediately behind him. As the camera continued the telecast, the newscaster fled leaving the two witnesses faces staring out of the television. In unison the two preachers proclaimed in a loud voice, "The first woe is past, two other woes are yet to come. Beware of the horsemen!" The camera went dark as people wondered what the cryptic message could mean.

The department of defense called an emergency meeting. Satellite imagery had detected some unusual activity surrounding southern Iraq and the northern Arabian Peninsula. Early images depicted a dark cloud which seemed to form over the region. As satellites were repositioned and clearer images obtained, it was discovered that this cloud was actually a horde of creatures that seemed to be growing from around the Euphrates River. Larger and larger the mass of creatures became. As scientists began to zoom onto the staggering crowd of creatures, they were astounded at what they saw.

These creatures were actually mounted troops but unlike any troops of this earth. The horses were the size of small elephants and their heads were large with powerful jaws and teeth like a lion. Instead of hair, their tails were like snakes each having claw-like teeth on the end. But out of the "horses" mouths came molten lava as the beasts seemed to cough. The riders upon these beasts were shadowy figures which had breastplates across their chests emblazoned with bright crimson, yellow and blue markings. The sheer number of these beasts were overwhelming. Some of the scientists estimated for this horde to cover the area revealed by the satellites, there had to be at least 200 million of these phenomenal beasts and riders.

While the scientists and strategists watched the live feeds from the satellite images, the cloud of the massive army began to move as the horde started to advance in all directions. Within hours masses of these incredible beasts began to be reported in Europe, Asia, and Africa. As they moved through cities and towns, the brimstone coming from the mouths of the beasts left massive destruction behind them. The antichrist mobilized his armies to intercept the invading horde. Batteries of artillery bombarded the invaders and fighter jets raged against the massive armies with missiles and bombs. However, as the smoke cleared, the invading beasts marched forward impervious to the onslaughts of the armies of the Antichrist. Within three weeks the beast armies had marched across the entire earth and were gone. Estimates were reported one in three people had been killed by the mounted horde.

The fear that had paralyzed the global population after the attack of the insect beasts turned into anger and rage at the onslaught of the beast armies. Although no one dared report it, criticisms and protests began to rumble throughout the world complaining their leader, the Antichrist, had been powerless to defend the world against the plagues of judgment sent by the terrorists in Jerusalem. An alert was sounded demanding the world's attention as the Antichrist would address the global population announcing new measures which would end the suffering once and for all.

As the world watched, the Antichrist announced he had discovered the terrorists in Jerusalem gained their spiritual power from the prayers of their followers who were scattered throughout the world in hiding. A new initiative was being immediately implemented. A mark of loyalty would be demanded of all citizens to be applied to their hand or forehead. This mark would be scanned before any business transactions could be conducted. No one would be able to buy or sell without the mark of loyalty. Any one refusing to take the mark of loyalty would be immediately executed. The Antichrist announced by the end of the month, all extremists would be annihilated. At the end of the month, without the power of their followers, the two terrorists would be defenseless. The Antichrist, himself, would lead the task force to arrest and execute these terrorists. The world cheered as the Antichrist announced the suffering would finally be over.

The whole world waited in expectation to see if the leader in whom they had trusted for nearly seven years would be able to finally usher in the peace he had promised. In anticipation, people began to attempt to get back to a normal state of life. Businesses began to open again, and the hustle of life seemed to revive. Long lines formed at "loyalty stations" where citizens could obtain the mark of loyalty. From time to time soldiers would arrive with a truck filled with captured dissidents, and they were herded into the loyalty stations to receive the mark. Those who refused were gunned down on the spot, and the bodies removed to make room for those who would follow their example. In businesses, scanners were installed, so patrons could confirm their loyalty marks before making purchases. Sometimes an alarm would sound when a shopper tried to pass through the scanner without the mark. If they could be detained before fleeing, they would be immediately taken by soldiers to the nearest loyalty station. Within two weeks, fewer trucks arrived and fewer alarms sounded. Posters and news reports proclaimed with pride the success of the loyalty marks.

The Seventh angel sounded his trumpet. After the overwhelming success of the loyalty marks, the Antichrist arrived in Jerusalem as promised. Surrounded by guards and soldiers, the Antichrist and his entourage made their way through the streets of Jerusalem and up to the temple mount. The two witnesses stood motionless; their eyes piercing through the crowds. TV cameras and media outlets surrounded the area for the entire world to watch what would happen. The Antichrist stood at a distance. His voice boomed over loud speakers, "Your followers are gone! You will no longer torment the world with your lies. Your days of terror are over!" The two preachers did not move. "Now the world will know who is really in charge," the Antichrist taunted.

He ordered the soldiers around him to arrest the terrorists. The soldiers started to move and then hesitated. The Antichrist railed, "Go! There is nothing more they can do to you!" The soldiers marched up the mount. The closer they got to the two witnesses the bolder they became. The soldiers grabbed the two witnesses and dragged them into the street in front of the Wailing Wall as the world watched. The crowd began screaming and cursing at the two men. The crowd grew quieter as the Antichrist announced over the loud speaker, "You have been found guilty of terrorism against the entire world. Your sentence is death!" The soldiers blindfolded the two men and the crowd backed away as a firing squad of soldiers assembled. The Antichrist shouted, "Fire!" and the two men crumpled to the ground.

The crowd and the watching world stood silent almost afraid to breathe waiting for their minds to conceive what had just happened. After a matter of seconds, someone in the crowd began to cheer and almost instantaneously thunderous applause roared over the crowd. From every corner of the world, as people saw the bodies of their tormentors lying in the street; cheering and shouts rang out. People everywhere partied and sent gifts to one another celebrating the deaths of the terrorists who had plagued them. The Antichrist had prevailed.

While everyone was still celebrating, an officer monitoring satellite feeds noticed something beginning to happen in the Middle East. A large group of people were on the move out of the country of Jordan. There was little concern about this group, strategists estimated there could be as many as 150,000 people. This was a large enough crowd to raise an alert, but not enough for alarm. However, something was odd about the images coming from the satellite. This mass of people were being led by a solitary figure, but the images of the leader were impossible to make out. Either a glitch in the cameras or some kind of interference made this leader look radiant, bleaching out the detail of his image. The vast crowd was clearly visible appearing like they were led by a burst of sunlight.

Further images revealed stragglers from the wilderness coming to join this multitude of people. Although the mass of people continually grew, the numbers were not large enough to cause concern. The distraction was duly noted, and this new development was added to official watch lists. The celebration of the victory over the terrorists continued.

The Jewish Remnant of 144,000

"Hello. My name is Razi. I lived in Jerusalem when the Antichrist demanded the world worship him. It is ironic the temple was built because of his influence in signing a treaty 3 ½ years ago, and now he sits in the temple claiming he is God. I am not a religious person, but every Jewish child is taught the *Shema Yisrael*, 'Hear, O Israel: the LORD our God, the LORD is one.' And, this man certainly is not the God of Israel. Jewish people have come to anticipate betrayal, and once again it had happened. With the Antichrist and his armies all over Jerusalem, we knew we had to flee. A great throng of people fled toward the East.

We had travelled a day's journey when the army of the Antichrist was seen in pursuit. Panic began to spread among us when the earth quaked and a chasm opened up and swallowed the pursuing army just as the Red Sea had swallowed the Egyptian army which had chased after our ancestors. We were amazed the God of Israel would once again protect His people; however, we knew we had to keep going. We found ourselves in the country of Jordan in the village of Bouseira. It was the ancient capital city of Edom once called Bozrah. No one really knows why we chose this place, but here we felt safe.

The first night in Bouseira, we went to sleep hungry. There were rumblings and murmurs among the people about how we would feed this multitude. By the time we settled down there were thousands of us here. Had we come into the wilderness just to die of hunger? When we awoke in the morning there was a snowy frost on the ground. This was quite remarkable because the temperatures even at night were quite warm. Many of us went out to investigate the frost and discovered rather than snow or frost, the ground was covered with bread. It was an unusual bread. It was sweet and filling. After we ate the bread, our energy level rose dramatically. It felt like you could run kilometers without breaking a sweat. It dawned on all of us at almost the same time; we were eating manna just as our forefathers had eaten when they wandered in the wilderness. Many voiced praise to the God of Abraham, Issac, and Jacob.

After we had been in Bouseira for quite some time, about mid-day we were going about our daily activities when the sun went dark. Some thought we were experiencing an eclipse. The moon became visible and turned as red as blood. The stars of the sky seemed to fly away as a light burst forth brighter than the sun had been. We all watched as One who looked like the Son of God appeared on the clouds. His brightness was so incredible, and a feeling of holiness settled over us with so much intensity we all fell to our faces. It was not a choice we made; it was the only action possible. We were still on our faces when the light subsided, and we rose in wonder of what had just happened. It was then; the Teacher showed up.

There was nothing special about Him. He came into our midst and began teaching from the law and the prophets about how the Messiah would come. As he spoke, his words burned within us. Everyone was drawn to this Teacher. For hours every day He would sit and teach and answer questions. Why He chose me I cannot say, but after a while He came to me and began talking one on one about the scriptures. He seemed to choose me as His disciple, and I could not refuse.

We spent hours and days and weeks together. I began feeling unworthy that He should spend so much time with me when there were others much more deserving. One day, I was talking to a group of friends, and one young man commented how the Teacher was spending too much time with him. Others said the same, and we all realized and wondered how He could have the time to personally teach each one of us.

I cannot tell if it was my imagination or the manna, but the more we listened to the Teacher; the more radiant He seemed to become. For months He had lived with us and taught us. Now, when we would gather together it was difficult to see His face. You had to shade your eyes to be able to see Him. Then, came the day when He called us all together. 'My brothers,' He said, 'I have been teaching you what the scriptures have said; the Messiah would come, and He has. He was the stone the builder's rejected; who has become the chief cornerstone. And now, I have returned to reclaim the lost sheep of Israel.'

As He spoke, we couldn't understand why we had not seen it before. The Teacher was the Anointed One, the Messiah. It was so obvious! Why did we not realize it sooner? This was finally the One we had waited for: the Hope of Israel. Then He said, 'My name is Jesus of Nazareth!' As He said those words an enormous feeling overwhelmed us. We were broken-hearted.

Many began to weep. Why had we been so stubborn? We had all been taught for generations that the name of Jesus was accursed. Now, we wondered why we had not understood who Messiah was long ago. How could we have been so blind? It seemed so evident to us now. Tears began to flow from thousands upon thousands of eyes."

> **Zech 12:10** (NIV) "And I will pour out on the house of David and the inhabitants of Jerusalem a spirit of grace and supplication. They will look on me, the one they have pierced, and they will mourn for him as one mourns for an only child, and grieve bitterly for him as one grieves for a firstborn son."

"At the mention of the name 'Jesus,' there were a few who puffed up with pride and shouted, 'we will never follow Jesus!' Even with the extreme brightness of His glory, for that is what we now saw, you could still see His eyes which filled with grief. He spoke tenderly to those who stood defiant. 'Oh Jerusalem, Jerusalem, how many times I would have gathered you under my wings as a hen gathers her chicks, but you would not let me.' He paused before He continued. 'We will be leaving to return to the Holy City. You may remain here, but you will never again enter the land of promise.' Many now began crying openly."

> **Ezekiel 20:35** And I will bring you into the wilderness of the people, and there will I plead with you face to face. 36 Like as I pleaded with your fathers in the wilderness of the land of Egypt, so will I plead with you, saith the Lord GOD. 37 And I will cause you to pass under the rod, and I will bring you into the bond of the covenant: 38 And I will purge out from among you the rebels, and them that transgress against me: I will bring them forth out of the country where they sojourn, and

they shall not enter into the land of Israel: and ye shall know that I am the LORD.

"In spite of the brokenness we felt, the other emotion which began to wash over us was joy. This was not a casual happiness. It was a deep inner surge which burst forth into a flood so real you could almost reach out and touch it. I cannot explain how sorrow and joy can mix, but it did in those moments, and it was held together by the glory of the Savior of Israel. The Teacher, Jesus, turned to the multitude and announced, 'My brothers, make ready for tomorrow we march to Jerusalem!'

The excitement was so widespread everyone was up and ready to go by dawn. The Lord Jesus led the way out of Bouseira, west toward Jerusalem. The mass of Jewish followers trailed behind Him as far as the eye could see."

> **Micah 2:12** (NIV) "I will surely gather all of you, O Jacob; I will surely bring together the remnant of Israel. I will bring them together like sheep in a pen, like a flock in its pasture; the place will throng with people. 13 One who breaks open the way will go up before them; they will break through the gate and go out. Their king will pass through before them, the LORD at their head."

"The journey to Jerusalem would be a hard three day walk. But as we journeyed, no one felt fatigue. We were like children who couldn't wait to go to the park to run and play. It was amazing just to listen to the excited chatter as we marched along, and then, to glance forward and see the magnificent glory of the King of Kings leading the way.

As we travelled toward Jerusalem, people began to come from all around us joining our procession. Many times the Lord had to stop because from everywhere people would gather and be sitting all over the road weeping and wailing begging for forgiveness from the One they had rejected. Jesus was so compassionate with these converts.

He would tell them to come and walk with Him, and before long you could see them laughing and rejoicing. Hour by hour the multitude that followed Jesus grew. Many Gentiles came and joined our procession. It seemed the farther we journeyed; the more people came to follow the Lord. On the third day we entered the Holy City."

> **Hosea 11:10-11** (NIV) They will follow the LORD; he will roar like a lion. When he roars, his children will come trembling from the west. {11} "They will come trembling like birds from Egypt, like doves from Assyria. I will settle them in their homes," declares the LORD.

"Walking into the city of Jerusalem we were surprised at the commotion. People were out in the streets partying and dancing. The revelry continued as we walked onto the streets. When Jesus passed the crowds of people shouting and singing, they stopped and became quiet. His radiance shined forth, and they stood back in awe. As we continued into the city, the crowds parted like the wake of a ship, and soon all we could hear was the sound of our own footsteps.

The Lord Jesus led us up toward the temple mount where we came to the street leading to the Wailing Wall. There in the street were two dead bodies crumpled together in a pile. The stale wounds and dried blood revealed the men had been killed and left for dead. A cloud of flies buzzed around the bodies and the pungent smell of death drifted through the air. Jesus walked forward from the multitude a few paces, and then raised His hand and spoke in a loud voice, 'Behold the two Olive Trees, the two lampstands that stand before the Lord of the earth.' When He had spoken the two men stood up on their feet. There was no longer any sign of wounds or decay on them. Jesus lowered His hand, and suddenly, a voice thundered from heaven saying, 'Come up here!' A mist began to form around the feet of the two witnesses turning into a cloud that began to rise

31

lifting the two men into the sky. While the men rose the ground began to shake violently and in the distance buildings began to collapse. The people of the city fled from the chaos and soon the streets were deserted except for the followers of Christ. The Lord Jesus turned and began to walk down another street as the multitude followed Him. We walked to the Eastern side of the city, and stopped at the Church of the Mount of Olives.

Jesus continued to ascend the mountain. When He reached the top, the ground again began to shake and an earthquake split the Mount of Olives in half. In the crevasse where the mount had been was the opening to a vast cavern. The Lord Jesus spoke, 'Go, my people, enter your rooms and shut the doors behind you; hide yourselves for a little while until his wrath has passed by.'[1] The Lord Jesus had taught us about this place of protection prepared for this very hour. It was a place called Azel. As we entered the cavern mixed emotions flooded our hearts. There was a peace knowing God loved His people and desired to protect us, and yet a foreboding knowing that it meant God's punishment upon the rest of the world. When the last of our company had entered the cavern, the ground shook as the mountain closed behind us."

*****

The Mount of Olives looked as it had before except for the glory radiating from the One who stood at the top. The voice that had spoken before coming from heaven spoke again, "The kingdom of the world has become the kingdom of our Lord, and of his Christ; and he will reign for ever and ever."[2]

The Bowl Judgments

> **Revelation 15:1** And I saw another sign in heaven, great and marvelous, seven angels having the seven last plagues; for in them is filled up the wrath of God.

32

The first angel went and poured out his bowl. The next day after the earthquake had struck the city of Jerusalem, it was estimated that ten percent of the city had been severely damaged. There had been reports of a huge throng of protesters that had entered the city just before the earthquake, but if they had been there they had since disappeared. Disaster cleanup had already begun and people were scurrying about in an effort to deal with the aftermath of the quake. Road crews were working where a building had collapsed, and a large loader was filling a dump truck to haul off the debris. Suddenly, the driver stopped the large machine and fell out on the ground screaming. Ugly sores had broken out all over his body. Emergency workers rushed in an attempt to help the man when people all around began to cry out. The emergency workers, themselves, began to break out in huge blisters erupting everywhere on their bodies.

Within hours reports were coming in from all over the world of the pandemic afflicting everyone. Drugs seemed to have little effect, and each sore was excruciatingly painful. There didn't seem to be a single person who had not contracted the disease. The centers for disease control worked feverously in spite of their own pain to find a cure. The only people that seemed immune were those who had fled to remote areas and had not taken the mark of loyalty.

The second angel poured out his bowl. Three days later, news reporters appeared on television with a global alert. The sores could be seen on their arms and faces, as they reported that the poisoning of the Pacific Ocean had spread and all of the salt seas on earth had now turned to blood. Every living creature in the seas was dead. Mountains of sea creatures were washing up on the shores of the world. In despair, people began to wonder how mankind would survive.

The third angel poured out his bowl. Within hours, frantic reports were circulating how the saltwater poisoning had spread to freshwater streams and rivers. It was estimated within five days there would be no more sources of fresh water. People began to panic and riots broke out. Widespread looting and vandalism were prevalent. Armies were dispatched but had little effect against the global bedlam.

The fourth angel poured out his bowl. NASA alerts sounded once again. Another solar flare had been detected, but this flare dwarfed the largest ever recorded. Within hours temperatures began to rise. Even at night the sky was bright. Sunscreen sold out and still did not prevent scorching burns on anyone who ventured outside. Air conditioners could not handle the intense heat and failed consistently. Wildfires burned everywhere. Buildings burst into flames and were left to burn because of the water shortage. Automobiles were impossible to drive without the engines immediately overheating. There was nowhere to go and no way to escape the hopeless conditions. There were frequent reports of people committing suicide: jumping out of buildings, or walking out into the streets and shooting themselves. It became the only relief available.

The fifth angel poured out his bowl. After five days, the solar flares subsided and the heat began to decrease. The night brought a welcome drop in temperature; however, the next morning the sun did not rise. The darkness continued and became overwhelming. Hours upon hours of continued darkness became depressing and seemed to highlight the misery of the past weeks. The heat of the past few days had exacerbated the painful sores still erupting on every inch of skin. Four days of darkness continued which felt like weeks. Then, the sun came out again.

The sixth angel poured out his bowl. As sunlight filled the skies, it seemed the sores began to dissipate. News reports joyously reported that all over the world the pandemic seemed to be getting better. There was still a shortage of fresh water and rotting debris of the oceans were creating severe health hazards. However, the heat was gone, the darkness was gone, and the sores were better. On another front, there was a strange occurrence in the Middle East. It appeared the Euphrates River

34

had dried up. This was probably due to the fresh water shortage which still plagued the world.

The next day an alert was sounded to inform the world the Antichrist had once again found the solution to the world's problems. He would be making a global announcement that evening. Every person in the world watched as their leader began to speak. "Everyone remembers how I dealt with the two terrorists that had plagued our world for months. I had discovered they obtained spiritual power from the prayers of their followers. When we got rid of all those who followed them, they became powerless. Now, I must confess; although, we had dealt them a severe blow, I had failed to find the real source of their power.

Yes. The prayers of their followers were a significant element of their power. But, I have now discovered the true power we have been fighting against was not in the terrorists' prayers, but in the one they worship. These terrorists worship Jesus. We used to call them Christians, but they have become extinct. Their Jesus is fighting to hold on to the last vestiges of His power. But He has lost. He was crucified the first time He came, and we will do worse this time!" At these words citizens throughout the world jumped to their feet and shouted battle cries cursing the name of Jesus. The Antichrist continued, "I am calling out this Jesus for a showdown! I am calling on all nations to send their armies to the Middle East to the valley of Meggido. We will assemble there in eight days and put an end to Jesus so He will never afflict us again!" Again, angry shouts rang out from every part of the world.

> **Rev 16:13** (NIV) Then I saw three evil spirits that looked like frogs; they came out of the mouth of the dragon, out of the mouth of the beast and out of the mouth of the false prophet. 14 They are spirits of demons performing miraculous signs, and they go out to

the kings of the whole world, to gather them for the battle on the great day of God Almighty.

The next day all the leaders of the nations of the earth issued orders for their armies to begin deployment. Day and night cargo planes and jets continued to descend upon the Middle East. Masses of soldiers, artillery, and weapons of all kinds were unloaded and moved to the valley of Megiddo. All over the world, recruiting stations had lines of people that stretched for blocks as citizens of all ages were determined to help end the suffering and terrorism once and for all. The name of Jesus was spoken with hatred as millions of hearts were sworn on revenge.

On the eighth day, the largest army ever assembled stood in battle array across the vast valley. The multitude of soldiers was so massive it stretched up the side of the mountains that bordered the valley. Huge armaments, tanks, armored vehicles dotted the landscape. At the head of the valley stood the Antichrist. A dry smile stretched across his lips as he surveyed the valley. The largest mass of people ever seen by man sprawled out before him. Millions upon millions of armed soldiers arrayed the landscape. No doubt remained within him; he was now invincible against any foe.

The morning sun glistened from billions of mirrored surfaces across the valley. Millions of faces waited expectantly for the command of their leader. On the Eastern horizon a tear seemed to rip through the expanse of heaven as brightness burst forth dimming the light of the sun. The entire valley lit up as if on fire because of the brightness that exploded across the sky. From the middle of the brightness came a radiant multitude. They rode on white horses and the robes flowing behind them were ablaze. Their leader rode a magnificent white horse and his crimson robe looked as if it were dipped in blood. His eyes looked like they were on fire and upon his head were golden crowns.

As the armies of heaven descended, the pride on the faces of the multitude gathered in the valley changed to looks of terror. Confusion and fear spread across the army of the Antichrist. Blinded by the brightness of the host of heaven they began to attack and kill each other. Those still standing looked at one another as their faces burst into flame. In mere seconds the armies of Antichrist were decimated and the angelic soldiers seized the Antichrist and his false prophet, and they were thrown alive into the lake of fire.

> **Isaiah 13:8** (NIV) Terror will seize them, pain and anguish will grip them; they will writhe like a woman in labor. They will look aghast at each other, their faces aflame.

The seventh angel poured out his bowl. The earth began to shake and from every corner of the earth the sky lit up lightning and thunder. The loud voice came from heaven once more and shook the earth as it proclaimed, "It is done!" The shaking continued and became more and more violent. As the earth wrenched and twisted, mountains began to crumble and continents began to slide into the sea. The tides began to rise and islands were submerged. The cities of the nations' fell and Jerusalem, itself, was split into three parts. Huge hailstones the size of boulders fell from the sky, and those left upon the earth cursed God because the plague of hail was so terrible.

The voice from heaven shook the earth again, "If anyone worships the beast and his image and receives his mark on the forehead or on the hand, he, too, will drink of the wine of God's fury, which has been poured full strength into the cup of his wrath. He will be tormented with burning sulfur in the presence of the holy angels and of the Lamb. And the smoke of their torment rises for ever and ever. There is no rest day or night for those who worship the beast and his image, or for anyone who receives the mark of his name."[3]

Matt 25:31 When the Son of man shall come in his glory, and all the holy angels with him, then shall he sit upon the throne of his glory: 32 And before him shall be gathered all nations: and he shall separate them one from another, as a shepherd divideth his sheep from the goats.

The Lord Jesus Christ took His place to reign for 1,000 years from Mount Zion. The nations of the earth were gathered before the Lamb of God. He separated them like a shepherd separates the sheep from the goats. He put the sheep on His right hand, and to them He spoke. "Come, you who are blessed by my Father; take your inheritance, the kingdom prepared for you since the creation of the world."[4] He placed the goats on His left hand, and to them He said, "Depart from me, you who are cursed, into the eternal fire prepared for the devil and his angels."[5]

Before We Leave the Story

Artistic license has been taken with the prior narrative to imagine how the events could unfold. The circumstances were imagined, but the events themselves and the order in which they occur come directly from the scripture.

---

[1] Isaiah 26:20 (NIV)
[2] Revelation 11:15 (NIV)
[3] Revelation 14:9-11 (NIV)
[4] Matthew 25:34 (NIV)
[5] Matthew 25:41 (NIV)

Chapter 2
The Millennium

Christ predicted His return to the earth over two-thousand years ago. Along with the prediction, He spoke of a time when He would return to rule the earth for 1,000 years. The prediction of the 1,000 year or millennial reign of Christ is most explicitly found in the book of Revelation chapter 20 verses 1 through 7.

> **Rev 20:1** And I saw an angel come down from heaven, having the key of the bottomless pit and a great chain in his hand. 2 And he laid hold on the dragon, that old serpent, which is the Devil, and Satan, and **bound him a thousand years**, 3 And cast him into the bottomless pit, and shut him up, and set a seal upon him, that he should deceive the nations no more, **till the thousand years should be fulfilled**: and after that he must be loosed a little season. 4 And I saw thrones, and they sat upon them, and judgment was given unto them: and I saw the souls of them that were beheaded for the witness of Jesus, and for the word of God, and which had not worshipped the beast, neither his image, neither had received his mark upon their foreheads, or in their hands; and they lived and **reigned with Christ a thousand years**. 5 But the rest of the dead lived not again **until the thousand years were finished**. This is the first resurrection. 6 Blessed and holy is he that hath part in the first resurrection: on such the second death hath no power, but they shall be priests of God and of Christ, and shall **reign with him a thousand years**. 7 And when the **thousand years are expired**, Satan shall be loosed out of his prison (emphasis added)[1]

The question facing interpreters of these predictions is: When and what is the millennial reign of Christ and how does it fit in with His return for His people? The Millennium is the event predicted in scripture when Jesus Christ will rule this earth for 1,000 years. The Millennium is the starting point for understanding end-time prophecy. Many people will claim to have a certain "millennial" position such as "pre-millennial" or "post-millennial." These descriptions explain the relation between Christ's return to earth and the millennial reign as predicted in scripture.

The Millennium vs. Christ's Return

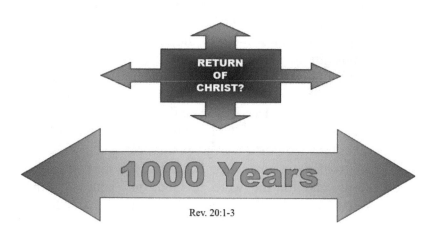

Figure 1: The Millennium

There are three major interpretations when the millennial reign will occur in relation to the return of Christ. These three are the A-millennial view, the post-millennial view and the Pre-millennial view. These three views cover the majority of opinion regarding the interpretation of the millennium during which Christ will rule.

A-millennial View

Post Millennial View

Pre-Millennial View

It is important to note, none of these views is universal or definitive. If you found two people who claim to be "A-Millennialists," you will most likely find they will still have significant differences in their interpretations. The following descriptions are typical of those holding each of these views.

A-Millennial View

The first view is called the A-Millennial View. The "Ah" in the Greek language is a form of negation, so the name "A-Millennial" means "No Millennium." The view is probably one of the more prevalent views today, particularly in the scholarly realm. Because of the problems of interpreting all the prophecies surrounding the return of Christ, many have chosen, to view the millennium as figurative or symbolic. They also view most of the book of Revelation in the same way. Those who hold to this view do not interpret the millennium as a literal span of time, but as prophetic of Heaven. They believe the world will get progressively worse until Christ returns, and the millennium will be the reality of heaven. The A-Millennial view is at some point in the future, Christ will return and the "millennium" will be our eternity in heaven.

Post-Millennial View

The Post Millennial view was much more prominent in previous generations than it is now. It is sometimes called the

Preterist View. Those who interpret the millennium in this way see most of the book of Revelation as historical. The Post-Millennial view sees the millennium beginning at the fall of Jerusalem in 70 A.D. The millennium is thought to be symbolic of the age we are living in right now. Christ does not rule in a physical sense but in a spiritual sense. The emergence of the church has become the presence of Christ ruling during this age. They expect the world to evolve in to a "new heaven and a new earth." Things will continually get better until Christ comes to reign on earth. They typically see the millennium as a figurative amount of time and not as a literal 1,000 years. There are those who try to time the millennium as already having happened either from the time of the fall of Jerusalem, or some other event during the church age.

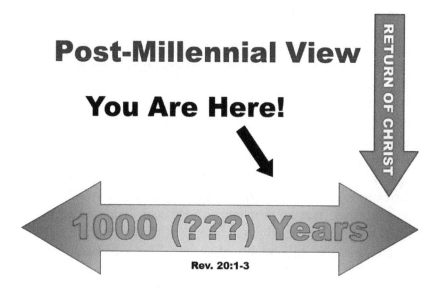

Figure 2: Post-Millennial View

Pre-Millennial View

The third view is called the Pre-Millennial View, and it is probably the most well-known and accepted among most people. It is the most literal interpretation of the scripture and views the millennium as a literal 1,000 years. The Pre-Millennial view sees the millennium as a future event preceded by a seven year period commonly known as the Tribulation Period. It is during this seven year time when God will judge the world and set up His millennial kingdom.

The Pre-Millennial View is depicted by the illustration in figure 3.

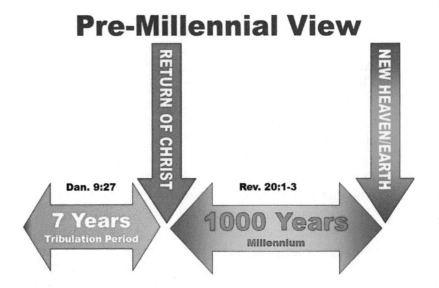

Figure 3: Pre-Millennial View

The Millennial reign of Christ will take place right after Christ returns to the earth. After the millennium, it is prophesied God will create a new heaven and a new earth. We are told in Revelation 21:1:

> **Rev 21:1** And I saw a new heaven and a new earth: for the first heaven and the first earth were passed away; and there was no more sea. **2** And I John saw the holy city, new Jerusalem, coming down from God out of

heaven, prepared as a bride adorned for her husband. **3** And I heard a great voice out of heaven saying, Behold, the tabernacle of God is with men, and he will dwell with them, and they shall be his people, and God himself shall be with them, and be their God. **4** And God shall wipe away all tears from their eyes; and there shall be no more death, neither sorrow, nor crying, neither shall there be any more pain: for the former things are passed away. **5** And he that sat upon the throne said, Behold, I make all things new. And he said unto me, Write: for these words are true and faithful.

According to the Pre-Millennial view, the millennial reign will be preceded by a seven year period prophesied in Daniel 9:27. This time has most commonly been called the "Tribulation Period." It is a name derived from scripture because the Bible does indicate that during this time there will be an intense period of trouble or tribulation. It is called in scripture "Tribulation" or the time of "Jacob's Trouble." There is some question about how the return of Christ will fit against these seven years. This is discussed in subsequent chapters.

This seven year period is most commonly called the "Tribulation Period," taken from passages like Matthew 24; however, a more accurate, scriptural name would be "Daniel's 70th Week." Daniel chapter 9 records future events about a ruler who is to come – whom we know as the Antichrist. Verse 27, states:

> **Daniel 9:27** (NIV) He will confirm a covenant with many for one `seven.' In the middle of the `seven' he will put an end to sacrifice and offering. And on a wing of the temple he will set up an abomination that causes desolation, until the end that is decreed is poured out on him.

This seven year period described by the prophet Daniel will precede the millennium. According to the Pre-Millennial View, all of these events are still in the future. We are still in a period commonly called the "church age." In Revelation 20:1-10, we have quite a detailed description of this thousand year period. This is why many hold to a more literal interpretation of the millennium, and this is the position of this study.

> **Rev 20:1** And I saw an angel come down from heaven, having the key of the bottomless pit and a great chain in his hand. **2** And he laid hold on the dragon, that old serpent, which is the Devil, and Satan, and bound him a **thousand years**, **3** And cast him into the bottomless pit, and shut him up, and set a seal upon him, that he should deceive the nations no more, till the **thousand years** should be fulfilled: and after that he must be loosed a little season. **4** And I saw thrones, and they sat upon them, and judgment was given unto them: and I saw the souls of them that were beheaded for the witness of Jesus, and for the word of God, and which had not worshipped the beast, neither his image, neither had received his mark upon their foreheads, or in their hands; and they lived and reigned with Christ a **thousand years**. **5** But the rest of the dead lived not again until the thousand years were finished. This is the first resurrection. **6** Blessed and holy is he that hath part in the first resurrection: on such the second death hath no power, but they shall be priests of God and of Christ, and shall reign with him a **thousand years**. **7** And when the **thousand years** are expired, Satan shall be loosed out of his prison, **8** And shall go out to deceive the nations which are in the four quarters of the earth, Gog and Magog, to gather them together to battle: the number of whom is as the sand of the sea. **9** And they went up on the breadth of the earth, and compassed the camp of the saints about, and the beloved city: and fire came down from God out of heaven, and devoured them. **10** And the devil that deceived them was cast into

the lake of fire and brimstone, where the beast and the false prophet are, and shall be tormented day and night for ever and ever (emphasis added).

An important point to note is: these three views of the millennium not only represent a difference in the viewpoint of end-time prophesy, but more importantly they reflect a difference in interpreting scripture. There is a fancy word which means "the science of interpreting scripture." It is the word "Hermeneutics" (Her-man-new-tics). The Apostle Paul wrote in **2 Corinthians 1:13** (NIV), "For we do not write you anything you cannot read or understand…" God gave us His Word so we could understand His purposes. So, how do we interpret scripture? These different views of the millennium reveal two basic ways to interpret the Bible.

The first is the allegorical method. The allegorical method sees everything as a symbol of something else. Both the A-Millennial and Post-Millennial views are allegorical interpretations. They see most prophecies as symbolic, and therefore the reader must determine the meaning of scripture. The literal method is to take the meaning of scripture in its most natural context.

According to Robert Van Kampen, in his book, *The Sign*, he suggests that there are five keys to a literal interpretation.[2]

FIVE KEYS FOR A LITERAL INTERPRETATION

1. Accept the meaning of scripture in its most normal, natural, and customary sense.

2. Take scripture in context.

3. Compare scripture with scripture.

4. *Before truth is realized, all seeming scriptural contradictions must be harmonized.*

5. *Watch for Near/Far prophetic applications in scripture.[3]*

The first four keys are self-explanatory, but the fifth key needs a little illustration. This is a common aspect of prophecy in the scriptures where a prophet describes an event, and that event takes place in the near future according to the prediction. Then, the prophecy is again fulfilled to a greater extent at a much later time in the future. An example of this concept is found in the book of Matthew where he quoted Isaiah's prophecy to King Ahaz...

> **Isaiah 7:14** Therefore the Lord himself shall give you a sign; Behold, a virgin shall conceive, and bear a son, and shall call his name Immanuel. 15 Butter and honey shall he eat, that he may know to refuse the evil, and choose the good. 16 For before the child shall know to refuse the evil, and choose the good, the land that thou abhorrest shall be forsaken of both her kings.

This prophecy was given to Ahaz and was fulfilled in his time. However, Matthew quotes this prophecy and applies it to the birth of Jesus.

> **Matt 1:22** Now all this was done, that it might be fulfilled which was spoken of the Lord by the prophet, saying, 23 Behold, a virgin shall be with child, and shall bring forth a son, and they shall call his name Emmanuel, which being interpreted is, God with us.

There were several hundred years between these two fulfillments. The first fulfillment was in the near future in King Ahaz's time, and the second fulfillment was in the far future when Jesus was born.

---

[1] All scriptural quotations are from the King James Version of the Bible unless otherwise noted.

[2] Robert Van Kampen, *The Sign* (Wheaton, IL: Crossway Books, 1999), 9.

[3] Ibid.

Chapter 3
Daniel's 70th Week

The first event of end-time prophecy is Daniel's 70th Week. As the name indicates, this week is described by the prophet Daniel.

> **Dan 9:24** Seventy weeks are determined upon thy people and upon thy holy city, to finish the transgression, and to make an end of sins, and to make reconciliation for iniquity, and to bring in everlasting righteousness, and to seal up the vision and prophecy, and to anoint the most Holy.

These "weeks" are sets of seven years. Therefore there are 70 sets of seven years prophesied. Daniel tells us the 70 "weeks" are determined regarding two things: 1) your people (Israel) and 2) your holy city (Jerusalem). Then he lists six goals for establishing this period of years:

---

1. To finish transgression

2. To put an end to sin

3. To reconcile wickedness

4. To bring in everlasting righteousness

5. To seal up vision and prophecy

6. To anoint the Most Holy

These six goals lead the reader to conclude God is revealing how He is going to complete His dealings with Israel and Jerusalem. In the next verse, he elaborates on this 70 "weeks" of years...

> **Daniel 9:25** Know therefore and understand, that from the going forth of the commandment to restore and to build Jerusalem unto the Messiah the Prince shall be **seven weeks**, and **threescore and two weeks**: the street shall be built again, and the wall, even in troublous times (emphasis added).

Daniel lists seven weeks, or sets of seven years, followed by threescore and two weeks: three twenties plus two or 62 sets of seven years. If we do the math, we discover from this verse that 69 sets of seven years, or 483 years, are predicted from the time the decree is issued to rebuild Jerusalem until the Messiah comes the first time.

(7 sevens + 62 sevens = 69 sevens)

69 X 7 years = 483 Years

In 445 B.C. Artaxerxes Longimanus issued a decree to rebuild Jerusalem (cf. Neh 2:5) from 445 B.C. to Jesus Triumphal Entry into Jerusalem = 483 years exactly![1]

Daniel continues the prophecy...

> **Dan 9:26** (NIV) "After the **sixty-two 'sevens,'** the Anointed One will be cut off and will have nothing. The people of the ruler who will come will destroy the city and the sanctuary. The end will come like a flood: War will continue until the end, and desolations have been decreed. 27 He will confirm a covenant with many for

one `seven.' In the middle of the `seven' he will put an end to sacrifice and offering. And on a wing [of the temple] he will set up an abomination that causes desolation, until the end that is decreed is poured out on him" (emphasis added).

According to Daniel, after the 62 sets of seven years, something interrupts this flow of 70 weeks of years. We are told that Messiah will be "cut off." Therefore, 69 sets of seven years will be finished after the coming of the Messiah the first time, and then there will be one set of seven years left – Daniel's 70th "week" of years.

69 sevens + 1 seven = 70th seven = Daniel's 70th Week

We are told in verse 27 the prince (KJV) or ruler (NIV) "that shall come" will confirm a covenant with "many" for one "week." Most agree this "prince" refers to the Antichrist. Therefore, the 70th Week of Daniel will begin by the signing of a seven-year covenant with the Antichrist and the "many." Most theologians also agree this will be a covenant of peace involving Israel and the "many." Isaiah writes of this covenant:

Isaiah 28:15 Because ye have said, We have made a covenant with death, and with hell are we at agreement; when the overflowing scourge shall pass through, it shall not come unto us: for we have made lies our refuge, and under falsehood have we hid ourselves:

It is called a covenant with death and hell, and Israel will depend on this covenant to keep them safe. This covenant will usher in the 70th Week of Daniel. "69 Weeks are past, and only the 70th week remains before 'everlasting righteousness' can be

51

brought to Israel and the most Holy One will be anointed, reclaiming rule over the earth from Satan."[2].

Daniel's 70th week is also referred to in the book of Revelation. Although the prophecies do not explicitly mention Daniel, the correlation is unmistakable.

> **Rev 13:4** And they worshipped the dragon which gave power unto the beast: and they worshipped the beast, saying, Who is like unto the beast? who is able to make war with him? **5** And there was given unto him a mouth speaking great things and blasphemies; and power was given unto him to continue forty and two months.

We are told that the "beast" will exercise his authority for 42 months – which is 3 ½ years or one-half of seven years. This corresponds to Daniel's prophecy relating to the "middle of the seven."

> **Daniel 9:27** (NIV) He will confirm a covenant with many for **one 'seven.'** In the **middle of the 'seven'** he will put an end to sacrifice and offering. And on a wing of the temple he will set up an **abomination that causes desolation**, until the end that is decreed is poured out on him (emphasis added).

---

42 months = 3 ½ years

3 ½ years = "the middle of the seven"

In the book of Revelation we are given the picture of the woman giving birth to a male child. Most theologians agree this "woman" symbolizes the nation of Israel who gives birth to the Messiah.

Rev 12:1 And there appeared a great wonder in heaven; a woman clothed with the sun, and the moon under her feet, and upon her head a crown of twelve stars: **2** And she being with child cried, travailing in birth, and pained to be delivered. **3** And there appeared another wonder in heaven; and behold a great red dragon, having seven heads and ten horns, and seven crowns upon his heads. **4** And his tail drew the third part of the stars of heaven, and did cast them to the earth: and the dragon stood before the woman which was ready to be delivered, for to devour her child as soon as it was born. **5** And she brought forth a man child, who was to rule all nations with a rod of iron: and her child was caught up unto God, and to his throne.

Revelation goes on to describe how the dragon pursues the woman; however, she is protected by God.

Rev 12:6 And the woman fled into the wilderness, where she hath a place prepared of God, that they should feed her there a thousand two hundred and threescore days.

1,260 Days = 3½ Years

Again, we have this 3 ½ year period mentioned. It is stated again differently in verse 14…

Rev 12:14 And to the woman were given two wings of a great eagle, that she might fly into the wilderness, into her place, where she is nourished for a time, and times, and half a time, from the face of the serpent.

Time (1 Year) + Times (2 Years) +

½ Time (½ Year) = 3½ Years

What we are seeing is the 70th Week of Daniel culminates in the last 3 ½ years after the Abomination of Desolation takes place. The prophet Daniel elaborates further on these time periods...

> **Dan 12:11** And from the time that the daily sacrifice shall be taken away, and the abomination that maketh desolate set up, there shall be a thousand two hundred and ninety days [1,290]. **12** Blessed is he that waiteth, and cometh to the thousand three hundred and five and thirty days [1,335] (numerical representations added).

The prophecy in Daniel now introduces two new numbers of days which represent an extra 30 days and 45 days respectively at the end of Daniel's 70th Week.

1,290 days = [1,260 days + 30 days]

1,335 days = [1,290 days + 45 days]

Daniel prophesies of "the middle of the seven" which is 3½ years or 1,260 days. Afterwards, he states from the time the Abomination of Desolation is set up - which is at the middle of the seven; there will be 1,290 days (this is 30 days more than the 3½ years). It continues "blessed is the one" (NIV) who reaches the 1,335 days. This is 45 more days than the 1,260 + 30. Rev. 13:5 tells us the Antichrist will rule for 42 months or 1,260 days. Daniel 9:27 states: the Abomination of Desolation will be set up until the "end that is decreed is poured out on him." At that point, we are told that one is blessed if he reaches the 1,335 days.

In summary, the Antichrist will rule for 1,260 days or 3 ½ years. Then the "end that is decreed" will be poured out on him 30 days later. Anyone who lasts until 45 more days after the Antichrist is "ended" is called blessed. Therefore, we can put together this picture as depicted in the chart below.

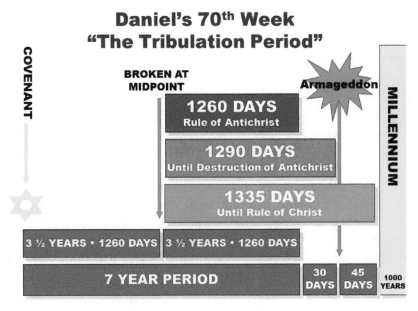

Figure 4: Tribulation Period

The Antichrist will rule until the end of the 70th week or 1,260 days. Thirty days later he will meet his "end." The book of Revelation tells us his "end" will be at Armageddon. The next event will be the establishment of the millennial reign of Christ which we can surmise will happen 45 days later.

Another of the major events which takes place at the end of Daniel's 70th week is the salvation of all Israel. The Apostle Paul states...

Rom 11:25 For I would not, brethren, that ye should be ignorant of this mystery, lest ye should be wise in your own conceits; that blindness in part is happened to Israel, until the fulness of the Gentiles be come in. **26** And **so all Israel shall be saved**: as it is written, There shall come out of Sion the Deliverer, and shall turn away ungodliness from Jacob: **27** For this is my covenant unto them, when I shall take away their sins (emphasis added).

The prophet Zechariah records by this time there will only be 1/3 of Israel left!

Zech 13:8 And it shall come to pass, that in all the land, saith the LORD, two parts therein shall be cut off and die; but the third shall be left therein. **9** And I will bring the third part through the fire, and will refine them as silver is refined, and will try them as gold is tried: they shall call on my name, and I will hear them: I will say, It is my people: and they shall say, The LORD is my God.

Now, we can modify our chart to include this last event of Daniel's 70th Week (figure 5), when all Israel will finally accept Jesus Christ as their true Messiah. This is foretold in Zechariah...

Zech 12:10 And I will pour upon the house of David, and upon the inhabitants of Jerusalem, the spirit of grace and of supplications: and they shall look upon me whom they have pierced, and they shall mourn for him, as one mourneth for his only son, and shall be in bitterness for him, as one that is in bitterness for his firstborn.

The Apostle Paul wrote...

Rom 11:23 (NIV) And if they do not persist in unbelief, they will be grafted in, for God is able to graft them in again.

In Romans 11:25 we are told that all Israel will be saved after the fullness of the Gentiles has come in. Revelation 11:2 states:

Revelation 11:2 (NIV) But exclude the outer court; do not measure it, because it has been **given to the Gentiles**. They will trample on the holy city **for 42 months** (emphasis added).

Therefore, we can conclude that all Israel will be saved at the end of Daniel's 70th Week or 42 months after the Abomination of Desolation.

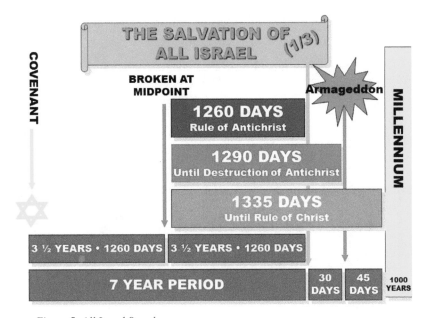

Figure 5: All Israel Saved

---

[1] Sir Robert Anderson, *The Coming Prince* (Grand Rapids: Kregel, 1972), iii.

[2] Van Kampen, 91.

Chapter 4
The 30 Days

There are two periods mentioned in the book of Daniel that occur immediately after the end of Daniel's 70th Week.

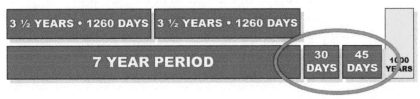

Figure 6: Two Periods

Robert Van Kampen names the 30 day portion as "The Reclamation Period[1]," and the 45 day portion he called "The Restoration Period[2]." These names are chosen to clarify the things that will happen during each specific period. To understand the 30 day Reclamation Period, we must look back at what will happen at the mid-point of the 70th Week.

The Antichrist is revealed and demands worship

The Woman flees to the wilderness

144,000 are sealed

Two Witnesses prophesy for 1,260 days

Trumpet Judgments Begin

Antichrist Demands Worship

The Antichrist will sign a seven year covenant with Israel and other nations. At the mid-point of the 70th Week, or 3½ years into the covenant, he will break the terms of the covenant and demand the world worship him.

> **Dan 9:27** (NIV) He will confirm a covenant with many for one 'seven.' In the middle of the 'seven' he will put an end to sacrifice and offering. And on a wing of the temple he will set up an abomination that causes desolation, until the end that is decreed is poured out on him.

The Apostle Paul records more clearly what this "Abomination of Desolation" will be...

> **2 Thess 2:3** Let no man deceive you by any means: for that day shall not come, except there come a falling away first, and that man of sin be revealed, the son of perdition; **4** Who opposeth and exalteth himself above all that is called God, or that is worshipped; so that he as God sitteth in the temple of God, shewing himself that he is God.

The prophet Daniel calls this event by the Antichrist the Abomination of Desolation and describes how he will be set up on a wing of the temple. The Apostle Paul also describes the Antichrist setting himself up in God's temple claiming that he, himself, is God. He goes on to say that he exalts himself above all that is worshipped. Therefore, when the Abomination of Desolation takes place, the Antichrist will demand the worship of the world.

Woman Flees to Wilderness

Next, the scripture tells us the "woman" will flee to the wilderness. Most theologians agree this woman is a symbol for Israel. The scripture records the woman will be supernaturally protected from the dragon who is identified in Revelation 12:9 as the devil.

> **Rev 12:13** And when the dragon saw that he was cast unto the earth, he persecuted the woman which brought forth the man child. **14** And to the woman were given two wings of a great eagle, that she might fly into the wilderness, into her place, where she is nourished for a time, and times, and half a time, from the face of the serpent.

So, the woman – Israel is protected out of the reach of the serpent for a time, times, and a half a time. This period of time is again mentioned and corresponds with the period of time from the Abomination of Desolation until the end of Daniel's 70th Week.

Time = 1 year; times = 2 years, ½ time = ½ year

1 + 2 + ½ = 3 ½ years

In Revelation 12:14 we are told that the woman's place of protection is in the wilderness. Scripture identifies this "wilderness" as the land of Edom. The prophet Obadiah prophesies against Edom for the way they will treat those of Israel who flee...

Obadiah 1:12 But thou shouldest not have looked on the day of thy brother in the day that he became a stranger; neither shouldest thou have rejoiced over the children of Judah in the day of their destruction; neither shouldest thou have spoken proudly in the day of distress. **13** Thou shouldest not have entered into the gate of my people in the day of their calamity; yea, thou shouldest not have looked on their affliction in the day of their calamity, nor have laid hands on their substance in the day of their calamity; **14** Neither shouldest thou have stood in the crossway, to cut off those of his that did escape; neither shouldest thou have delivered up those of his that did remain in the day of distress. **15** For the day of the LORD is near upon all the heathen: as thou hast done, it shall be done unto thee: thy reward shall return upon thine own head.

144,000 Are Sealed

We are told shortly after the Abomination of Desolation, 144,000 Jewish people are "sealed."

Rev 7:3 Saying, Hurt not the earth, neither the sea, nor the trees, till we have sealed the servants of our God in their foreheads. **4** And I heard the number of them which were sealed: and there were sealed an hundred and forty and four thousand of all the tribes of the children of Israel.

Most theologians agree this 144,000 identifies the "woman." Therefore, as Antichrist begins to demand the worship of the world, Israel will rebel and at least 144,000 will flee to a desert place prepared for them. The prophet Ezekiel describes a future time when God will deal directly with the Israelites.

Ezekiel 20:35 And I will bring you into the wilderness of the people, and there will I plead with you face to face. **36** Like as I pleaded with your fathers in the wilderness of the land of Egypt, so will I plead with you, saith the Lord GOD. **37** And I will cause you to pass under the rod, and I will bring you into the bond of the covenant: **38** And I will purge out from among you the rebels, and them that transgress against me: I will bring them forth out of the country where they sojourn, and they shall not enter into the land of Israel: and ye shall know that I am the LORD.

Placing this prophecy into the timeline of Daniel's 70th Week and the timing of the salvation of all Israel indicates that a part of Jesus' return will be to deal with the nation of Israel. The passage records, "there I will plead with you face to face." The implication is Jesus will deal personally with Israel, and they will accept Him as their true Messiah. Those who rebel will not be brought back to the land of Israel.

Two Witnesses Prophesy for 1,260 Days

That number - 1,260 days (or 3½ years) appears again as the book of Revelation foretells two servants of God that will come on the scene.

Rev 11:3 And I will give power unto my two witnesses, and they shall prophesy a thousand two hundred and threescore days, clothed in sackcloth. **4** These are the two olive trees, and the two candlesticks standing before the God of the earth. **5** And if any man will hurt them, fire proceedeth out of their mouth, and devoureth their enemies: and if any man will hurt them, he must in this manner be killed. **6** These have power to shut heaven, that it rain not in the days of their prophecy: and have power over waters to turn them to blood, and to smite the earth with all plagues, as often as they will.

These witnesses will be servants of God that will prophesy or testify during the time the Antichrist rules the earth. However, the Antichrist will have no power over these witnesses until the 3 ½ years of their testimony is completed. On the contrary, these witnesses will have power to not only to protect themselves, but to inflict various plagues upon the earth.

Many have sought to identify these two witnesses, the scripture doesn't explicitly tell us. However, common thought is these two could be Moses and Elijah. This identification is most likely based upon Moses dealing with the plagues of Egypt and Elijah shutting up the heavens from rain during his time as a prophet. Also, the prophet Malachi prophesied the coming of Elijah before the coming of the Day of the Lord.

> **Malachi 4:5** Behold, I will send you Elijah the prophet before the coming of the great and dreadful day of the LORD.

Trumpet Judgments Begin

> **Rev 8:1** And when he had opened the seventh seal, there was silence in heaven about the space of half an hour. **2** And I saw the seven angels which stood before God; and to them were given seven trumpets... **6** And the seven angels which had the seven trumpets prepared themselves to sound.

The trumpet judgments begin the outpouring of the wrath of God upon the earth. The trumpet judgments begin after God's wrath is said to have come after the opening of the sixth seal.

> **Revelation 6:12** And I beheld when he had opened the sixth seal, and, lo, there was a great earthquake; and the sun became black as sackcloth of hair, and the moon

became as blood... **17** For the great day of his wrath is come; and who shall be able to stand?

The opening of the sixth seal finishes chapter six of Revelation. Chapter seven describes the sealing of the 144,000 Jews and the multitude in heaven which no one can number from all nations, kindreds, peoples, and tongues. Chapter eight then begins to describe the trumpet judgments. Therefore, the narrative of judgment following the pronouncement of the day of wrath beginning at the end of chapter six is carried out by the trumpet judgments beginning in chapter eight.

As Daniel's 70th Week concludes, the 30 day reclamation period begins, and these events will lead into the final 30 and 45 day periods following the 70th Week.

75 Days Period

- ◆ **Salvation of the Remnant of Israel**
- ◆ **The Final Wrath of God**
- ◆ **The Bema Judgment**
- ◆ **The Battle of Armageddon**

30 DAYS

- ◆ **The Restoration of Mount Zion**
- ◆ **The Restoration of Israel**
- ◆ **The Restoration of the Temple**
- ◆ **Christ to Rule over the Earth**

45 DAYS

Figure 7: The 75 Days

We have completed an overview of the events that are prophesied to take place during the final 3 ½ years of Daniel's 70th Week. Much greater detail will be given to these prophesies and their timing further on - but, to understand the 75 days that follow the 70th Week, the background of prior events must be introduced. The 75 day period following the 70th Week is depicted in figure 7.

The 30 day Reclamation Period will consist of four major events which will serve to finalize God's judgment of the world. Furthermore, as the prophecies are calculated, so often giving the number of days, it is possible to set the timing of the 30 day period and to delineate what will happen during the first five days of this Reclamation Period.

Two Witnesses Killed

First, we can place the timing of the 30 day period because of the prophecy of the death of the two witnesses...

> **Rev 11:7** And when they shall have finished their testimony, the beast that ascendeth out of the bottomless pit shall make war against them, and shall overcome them, and kill them. **8** And their dead bodies shall lie in the street of the great city, which spiritually is called Sodom and Egypt, where also our Lord was crucified.

We were told in Rev. 11:3-6 the witnesses WILL testify for 1,260 days. Therefore, they cannot be killed until their testimony is finished. Furthermore, the death of the two witnesses is clearly foretold as occurring just before the seventh angel sounds his trumpet in Rev. 10:7. So, the timing is clarified by these two markers.

Cannot be killed until end of 1260 Days

Between 6th and 7th Trumpets

This places the timing clearly at the end of the 70th Week and the beginning of the 30 day period. Specifically, the witnesses are killed WHEN their testimony is finished. Therefore, they will be killed on the first day of the 30 day period.

All Israel Saved

Prophecies concerning the salvation of Israel also help pinpoint the timing of events during these 30 days. The Apostle Paul gives us a clue as to what will happen next...

> **Rom 11:25** For I would not, brethren, that ye should be ignorant of this **mystery**, lest ye should be wise in your own conceits; that blindness in part is happened to Israel, until the fulness of the Gentiles be come in. **26** And so **all Israel shall be saved**: as it is written, There shall come out of Sion the Deliverer, and shall turn away ungodliness from Jacob (emphasis added)

Paul is explaining all of Israel WILL be saved and he calls it specifically a "mystery." This exact same term is used in the book of Revelation as the seventh trumpet is about to sound.

> **Rev 10:7** But in the days of the voice of the seventh angel, when he shall begin to sound, the **mystery** of God should be finished, as he hath declared to his servants the prophets (emphasis added).

Therefore, the salvation of Israel will take place at the end of Daniel's 70th Week when the seventh trumpet is about to sound.

The prophet Hosea acknowledges the repentant spirit of Israel at the last day. He also provides us with a time frame for Israel's restoration back to their true Messiah.

Hosea 6:1 Come, and let us return unto the LORD: for he hath torn, and he will heal us; he hath smitten, and he will bind us up. **2 After two days** will he revive us: **in the third day** he will raise us up, and we shall live in his sight. **3** Then shall we know, if we follow on to know the LORD: his going forth is prepared as the morning; and he shall come unto us as the rain, as the latter and former rain unto the earth. (emphasis added).

So, the restoration of Israel will be a three day process. It is also interesting to note that Hosea states the Lord will appear and come to them. There are several prophecies which indicate the Lord will deal personally with Israel in the last day.

Micah 2:12-13 (NIV) "I will surely gather all of you, O Jacob; I will surely bring together the remnant of Israel. I will bring them together like sheep in a pen [Bozrah], like a flock in its pasture; the place will throng with people. {**13**} One who breaks open the way will go up before them; they will break through the gate and go out. Their king will pass through before them, **the LORD at their head**." (emphasis added)

The prophet Micah states Israel (or Jacob) will be gathered like sheep in a pen. The Hebrew word for pen is the word **Bozrah**. In fact, the King James Version of the Bible translates this verse as follows...

Micah 2:12 (KJV) ... I will put them together as the sheep of **Bozrah**, as the flock in the midst of their fold... (emphasis added)

The conclusion is Israel will flee to Edom and to the city of Bozrah. It is also important to note Micah 2:13 prophesies there is One who will go up before them... "Their King will pass through before them, the LORD at their head."

The Journey to Jerusalem

> **Isaiah 63:1-4** (NIV) Who is this coming from Edom, from Bozrah, with his garments stained crimson? Who is this, robed in splendor, striding forward in the greatness of his strength? "It is I, speaking in righteousness, mighty to save." {**2**} Why are your garments red, like those of one treading the winepress? {**3**} "I have trodden the winepress alone; from the nations no one was with me. I trampled them in my anger and trod them down in my wrath; their blood spattered my garments, and I stained all my clothing. {**4**} For the day of vengeance was in my heart, and the year of my redemption has come."

All of these prophesies indicate Jesus will personally appear to those Israelites who flee to Edom. He will judge them, and they will finally acknowledge Jesus Christ as their true Messiah and Lord. Afterwards, he will lead them out of Bozrah on a two day journey to Jerusalem. Other prophecies indicate the Edomite remnant will not be the only Israelites who come to the Lord. In addition to the Jews that flee to Edom, other Jewish people will flee in all directions to escape the persecution of the Antichrist. As Jesus leads the Edomite remnant to Jerusalem, He will be joined by other remaining Jews who have survived and are finally willing to recognize their true Messiah.

> **Hosea 11:10-11** (NIV) They will follow the LORD; he will roar like a lion. When he roars, his children will come trembling from the west. {**11**} "They will come trembling like birds from Egypt, like doves from Assyria. I will settle them in their homes," declares the LORD.

Those who come to Jesus from all over the world are called His children. Other passages indicate this will be a gathering of

69

all of those who are left - who finally accept Christ as their Savior. The indication is this will be a gathering that includes non-Jewish people who are ready to believe in Jesus as the true Messiah.

> **Isaiah 14:1** For the LORD will have mercy on Jacob, and will yet choose Israel, and set them in their own land: and the **strangers shall be joined with them**, and they shall cleave to the house of Jacob (emphasis added).

Thus, this seems to be a universal gathering of all those who believe in Jesus - what a reunion! One of the most moving scriptures about this time is found in Zechariah:

> **Zec 12:10** (NIV) And I will pour out on the house of David and the inhabitants of Jerusalem a spirit of grace and supplication. They will look on me, the one they have pierced, and they will mourn for him as one mourns for an only child, and grieve bitterly for him as one grieves for a firstborn son.

As Jesus makes His way to Jerusalem, a multitude of the Israelites and Gentiles will come flocking to Him - recognizing He is Lord. Furthermore, something awesome happens! On the third day, Jesus enters Jerusalem. This is also the day prophesied when the two witnesses are resurrected. The Antichrist will kill the two witnesses on the first day of the 30 day period, and their bodies will lie in the streets for three days.

> **Rev 11:10** And they that dwell upon the earth shall rejoice over them, and make merry, and shall send gifts one to another; because these two prophets tormented them that dwelt on the earth. **11** And after three days and an half the Spirit of life from God entered into them, and they stood upon their feet; and great fear fell upon them which saw them.

The scripture is not explicit, but the prophecies lead one to believe that Jesus, Himself, arrives in Jerusalem with redeemed Israel and raises the two witnesses from the dead. What a spectacular possibility! Three days have a significant meaning in scripture. Jesus was in the grave for three days after the crucifixion before He was resurrected. When God prepared to appear to the children of Israel in the wilderness, He had them consecrate themselves for three days.

> **Exodus 19:10** And the LORD said unto Moses, Go unto the people, and sanctify them today and tomorrow, and let them wash their clothes, **11** And be ready against the third day: for the third day the LORD will come down in the sight of all the people upon mount Sinai.

Israel was to take three days to be ready to meet the Lord. It seems fitting in three days; all Israel is saved and the two witnesses are resurrected. Prophecy tells us once He arrives in Jerusalem, Jesus will lead Israel to Mount Zion, because He is reclaiming His rule over the earth.

> **Obadiah 1:21** And saviours shall come up on mount Zion to judge the mount of Esau; and the kingdom shall be the LORD'S.

> **Revelation 14:1** And I looked, and, lo, a Lamb stood on the mount Sion, and with him an hundred forty and four thousand, having his Father's name written in their foreheads... **3** And they sung as it were a new song before the throne, and before the four beasts, and the elders: and no man could learn that song but the hundred and forty and four thousand, which were redeemed from the earth. **4** ...These were redeemed from among men, being the firstfruits unto God and to the Lamb.

At this point the seventh angel sounds his trumpet...

Rev 11:15 And the seventh angel sounded; and there were great voices in heaven, saying, The kingdoms of this world are become the kingdoms of our Lord, and of his Christ; and he shall reign for ever and ever.

This passage denotes the beginning of another of the six major events reviewed in chapter one: God reclaiming rule of this earth. But God's judgment is not quite over...

Rev 14:7 Saying with a loud voice, Fear God, and give glory to him; for the hour of his judgment is come: and worship him that made heaven, and earth, and the sea, and the fountains of waters.

Rev 14:19 And the angel thrust in his sickle into the earth, and gathered the vine of the earth, and cast it into the great winepress of the wrath of God. **20** And the winepress was trodden without the city, and blood came out of the winepress, even unto the horse bridles, by the space of a thousand and six hundred furlongs.

Rev 15:1 And I saw another sign in heaven, great and marvellous, seven angels having the seven last plagues; for in them is filled up the wrath of God.

God's final wrath is about to be poured out on the world, and it will happen swiftly. Revelation describes the seven bowl judgments that follow the seven trumpets. But before these final judgments are poured out, Jesus provides for His followers.

Zechariah 14:4 And his feet shall stand in that day upon the mount of Olives, which is before Jerusalem on the east, and the mount of Olives shall cleave in the midst thereof toward the east and toward the west, and there shall be a very great valley; and half of the mountain shall remove toward the north, and half of it toward the south. **5** And ye shall flee to the valley of the mountains; for the valley of the mountains shall reach unto **Azal**: yea, ye shall flee, like as ye fled from before the earthquake in the days of Uzziah king of Judah: and the LORD my God shall come, and all the saints with thee.

In this prophecy, God has prepared a place of refuge for His people before His final wrath is poured out. This is the only place Azel (NIV) is mentioned, and we know nothing more about it except it is a place of refuge. A passage in Isaiah references this time of protection:

> **Isaiah 26:20-21** (NIV) Go, my people, enter your rooms and shut the doors behind you; hide yourselves for a little while until his wrath has passed by. {21} See, the LORD is coming out of his dwelling to punish the people of the earth for their sins. The earth will disclose the blood shed upon her; she will conceal her slain no longer.

As with Noah and Lot, when God's people are in a place of protection; God's wrath is poured out. The bowl judgments begin:

> **Rev 16:1** (NIV) Then I heard a loud voice from the temple saying to the seven angels, "Go, pour out the seven bowls of God's wrath on the earth."

Knowing the timing of these few events allows us to assemble an idea of what the beginning of the 30 day reclamation period will look like. Therefore, the events of the first five days of the 30 day period are depicted in figure 8.

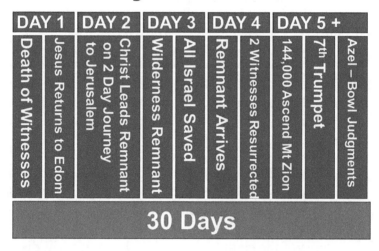

Figure 8: 30 Day Reclamation

The Bowl Judgments

The bowl judgments are God's final expression of judgment. They differ from the trumpet judgments in the following ways:

They will happen quickly (possibly in as little as 25 days)

All things affected (rather than 1/3 as in the trumpet judgments)

Seventh Bowl = Total Devastation

Followed by Armageddon

The bowl judgments are God's final wrath and because of their severity; they will happen rapidly and affect all things. They will culminate in the battle of Armageddon. The Bowl Judgments are described in the 16th chapter of the book of Revelation.

> **Rev 16:1** And I heard a great voice out of the temple saying to the seven angels, Go your ways, and pour out the vials of the wrath of God upon the earth. **2** And the first went, and poured out his vial upon the earth; and there fell a noisome and grievous sore upon the men which had the mark of the beast, and upon them which worshipped his image. **3** And the second angel poured out his vial upon the sea; and it became as the blood of a dead man: and every living soul died in the sea. **4** And the third angel poured out his vial upon the rivers and fountains of waters; and they became blood. **5** And I heard the angel of the waters say, Thou art righteous, O Lord, which art, and wast, and shalt be, because thou hast judged thus. **6** For they have shed the blood of saints and prophets, and thou hast given them blood to drink; for they are worthy. **7** And I heard another out of the altar say, Even so, Lord God Almighty, true and righteous are thy judgments. **8** And the fourth angel poured out his vial upon the sun; and power was given unto him to scorch men with fire. **9** And men were scorched with great heat, and blasphemed the name of God, which hath power over these plagues: and they repented not to give him glory. **10** And the fifth angel poured out his vial upon the seat of the beast; and his kingdom was full of darkness; and they gnawed their tongues for pain, **11** And blasphemed the God of heaven because of their pains and their sores, and repented not of their deeds. **12** And the sixth angel poured out his vial upon the great river Euphrates; and the water thereof

was dried up, that the way of the kings of the east might be prepared. **13** And I saw three unclean spirits like frogs come out of the mouth of the dragon, and out of the mouth of the beast, and out of the mouth of the false prophet. **14** For they are the spirits of devils, working miracles, which go forth unto the kings of the earth and of the whole world, to gather them to the battle of that great day of God Almighty. **15** Behold, I come as a thief. Blessed is he that watcheth, and keepeth his garments, lest he walk naked, and they see his shame. **16** And he gathered them together into a place called in the Hebrew tongue Armageddon. **17** And the seventh angel poured out his vial into the air; and there came a great voice out of the temple of heaven, from the throne, saying, It is done. **18** And there were voices, and thunders, and lightnings; and there was a great earthquake, such as was not since men were upon the earth, so mighty an earthquake, and so great. **19** And the great city was divided into three parts, and the cities of the nations fell: and great Babylon came in remembrance before God, to give unto her the cup of the wine of the fierceness of his wrath. **20** And every island fled away, and the mountains were not found. **21** And there fell upon men a great hail out of heaven, every stone about the weight of a talent: and men blasphemed God because of the plague of the hail; for the plague thereof was exceeding great.

As you read the bowl judgments, it becomes apparent they follow one another swiftly. For example, the first bowl is a judgment of sores. But, when the fifth bowl of darkness is poured out, the scripture states the people cursed God because of the sores - the sores were the first bowl. Therefore, the indication is there will not be much time in between judgments. It makes sense they would happen in a span of 25 days. Also, the fact all things are affected would necessitate that the bowls happen rapidly, or no one would be left alive. The second and third bowls turn the sea and fresh water into blood, and all living creatures in them die. Without the sea and fresh water, the inhabitants of the earth would not be able to survive long.

After the pouring out of God's final wrath in the form of the seven bowls, the 30 day period ends with two final events.

The Bema Judgment

The Battle of Armageddon

The Bema Judgment

By this time, all of the saints of God will be in heaven having been rescued from the earth in the "rapture." While the Salvation of Israel and God's final wrath are happening on earth; in heaven the saints of God will be undergoing what the scripture calls the "judgment seat of Christ." The word "judgment seat" is the Greek word "bêma." For that reason, this judgment is often called the "Bema Judgment." It is foretold by the Apostle Paul in 2 Corinthians:

> **2 Cor 5:10** For we must all appear before the judgment seat [bêma] of Christ; that every one may receive the things done in his body, according to that he hath done, whether it be good or bad. (Greek word added).

The timing of this judgment is revealed in Revelation 11:15-18 as being after the seventh trumpet has sounded.

> **Rev 11:15** And the seventh angel sounded; and there were great voices in heaven, saying, The kingdoms of this world are become the kingdoms of our Lord, and of

his Christ; and he shall reign for ever and ever. **16** And the four and twenty elders, which sat before God on their seats, fell upon their faces, and worshipped God, **17** Saying, We give thee thanks, O Lord God Almighty, which art, and wast, and art to come; because thou hast taken to thee thy great power, and hast reigned. **18** And the nations were angry, and thy wrath is come, and the time of the dead, that they should be judged, and that thou shouldest **give reward unto thy servants** the prophets, and to the saints, and them that fear thy name, small and great; and shouldest destroy them which destroy the earth (emphasis added).

There are three prophetic events mentioned in this passage. First, the seventh trumpet is sounded. Second, it is proclaimed God has once again begun to reign on earth. And third, the time has come for judging the dead and for rewarding God's servants. The reward of God's servants indicates the judgment seat of Christ will be taking place during this time.

We studied that there are 1,260 days for the rule of the Antichrist and 1,290 days until the destruction of the Antichrist. The question is: what happens to stop the rule of the Antichrist during the 30 days? Well, we have seen that Jesus, Himself, will return and lead the Israelites in exile back into Jerusalem and then reclaim rule from the Antichrist. With Jesus' return, the power of the Antichrist is limited. We are told this in the book of 2 Thessalonians.

> **2 Thessalonians 2:8** (NIV) And then the lawless one will be revealed, whom the Lord Jesus will overthrow with the breath of his mouth and destroy by the splendor of his coming.

The particular word *destroy* in the original language does not necessarily mean to annihilate, but to render ineffective.

Therefore, as Jesus appears on the scene, the Antichrist's power is rendered ineffective or limited.[3]

Dictionary entry:

ἀναιρέω

render ineffective, *nullify, cancel; destroy, abolish, do away with*
(passive pass away, cease);

Figure 9: anaireo

In fact, the only two actions we have recorded that the Antichrist will take during the 30 days, is to kill the two witnesses and to gather together the nations for the battle of Armageddon.

The Battle of Armageddon

The Battle of Armageddon is the final decisive battle against the Antichrist and the False Prophet. This is the event the prophet Daniel described when he predicted that after 1,290 days the end that has been decreed will be poured out on the Antichrist (Daniel 9:26). It is also another of the six major events introduced at the end of chapter one.

> **Rev 19:11** And I saw heaven opened, and behold a white horse; and he that sat upon him was called Faithful and True, and in righteousness he doth judge and make war. **12** His eyes were as a flame of fire, and on his head were many crowns; and he had a name written, that no man knew, but he himself. **13** And he was clothed with a vesture dipped in blood: and his name is called The Word of God. **14** And the armies which were in heaven followed him upon white horses,

clothed in fine linen, white and clean. **15** And out of his mouth goeth a sharp sword, that with it he should smite the nations: and he shall rule them with a rod of iron: and he treadeth the winepress of the fierceness and wrath of Almighty God. **16** And he hath on his vesture and on his thigh a name written, KING OF KINGS, AND LORD OF LORDS.

This is a description of the Lord Jesus leading the armies of heaven to the battle of Armageddon. This is the battle when the Antichrist will finally be defeated, and the war WILL be over! The scripture tells us that the Lord will be leading the armies of heaven.

Rev 19:13 And he was clothed with a vesture dipped in blood: and his name is called The Word of God. **14 And the armies which were in heaven followed him** upon white horses, clothed in fine linen, white and clean (emphasis added).

The question is: who are these "armies of heaven?" There are those who have asserted these armies include the saints of God who have been "raptured" into heaven. However, the scriptures are quite clear about the identity of this army.

Matt 13:40 As therefore the tares are gathered and burned in the fire; so shall it be in the end of this world. **41 The Son of man shall send forth his angels**, and they shall gather out of his kingdom all things that offend, and them which do iniquity; **42** And shall cast them into a furnace of fire: there shall be wailing and gnashing of teeth (emphasis added).

Here in Matthew, the scriptures tell us at the end of the age it will be the angels that are sent to "weed out" the kingdom.

Several other times the angels are spoken of as being the agents of divine judgment and completion.

> **2 Thess 1:7** And to you who are troubled rest with us, when the Lord Jesus shall be revealed from heaven **with his mighty angels, 8** In flaming fire taking vengeance on them that know not God, and that obey not the gospel of our Lord Jesus Christ (emphasis added).

The prophet Isaiah describes the devastating defeat the Antichrist and his followers will suffer.

> **Isaiah 34:1** Come near, ye nations, to hear; and hearken, ye people: let the earth hear... **2** For the indignation of the LORD is upon all nations, and his fury upon all their armies: he hath utterly destroyed them, he hath delivered them to the slaughter. **3** Their slain also shall be cast out, and their stink shall come up out of their carcases, and the mountains shall be melted with their blood.

Furthermore, the book of Revelation provides the details of the "end that has been decreed" regarding the Antichrist. He, along with the false prophet, will be cast into the lake of fire.

> **Rev 19:19** And I saw the beast, and the kings of the earth, and their armies, gathered together to make war against him that sat on the horse, and against his army. **20** And the beast was taken, and with him the false prophet that wrought miracles before him, with which he deceived them that had received the mark of the beast, and them that worshipped his image. **These both were cast alive into a lake of fire burning with brimstone. 21** And the remnant were slain with the sword of him that sat upon the horse, which sword proceeded out of his mouth: and all the fowls were filled with their flesh (emphasis added).

This passage deals with the aftermath of the battle. We are told the beast and the false prophet will be captured and thrown into the lake of fire. All the rest are killed by the sword which comes from the Lord's mouth. Some have speculated this "sword" is the Word of God coming from the mouth of Jesus. After all, in John 1:1 Jesus is called the Word.

---

[1] Van Kampen, 365.

[2] Ibid., 425.

[3] Barclay M. Newman, *A Concise Greek-English Dictionary of the New Testament* (London: United Bible Societies, 1971), 11.

Chapter 5
The 45 Days

The Restoration Period

There are four events which make up the final 45 days after Daniel's 70th Week or the Restoration Period.

The Restoration of Mount Zion

The Restoration of Israel

The Restoration of the Temple

Christ to Rule over the Earth[1]

With the final seventh bowl, God's judgment is finished as the last bowl is poured upon the earth.

> **Rev 16:17** And the seventh angel poured out his vial into the air; and there came a great voice out of the temple of heaven, from the throne, saying, It is done. **18** And there were voices, and thunders, and lightnings; and there was a great earthquake, such as was not since men were upon the earth, so mighty an earthquake, and so great. **19** And the great city was divided into three parts, and the cities of the nations fell: and great Babylon came in remembrance before God, to give unto her the cup of the wine of the fierceness of his wrath. **20** And every island fled away, and the mountains were not found.

The seventh bowl symbolizes total devastation. The earth will suffer a catastrophe as never before. It is described as the most severe earthquake which has ever taken place. The cities of the nations collapse; mountains and islands can no longer be found. One can understand why Jesus protects the saints in the place called Azel.

After the destruction of the seventh bowl is finished the 30 day Reclamation Period is over and the 45 day Restoration Period begins. The Restoration Period signifies the time span God uses to prepare the earth for the millennial kingdom ruled personally by Jesus Christ.

The Restoration of Mt. Zion

> **Zechariah 14:10** (NIV) The whole land, from Geba to Rimmon, south of Jerusalem, will become like the Arabah. But Jerusalem will be raised up and remain in its place, from the Benjamin Gate to the site of the First Gate, to the Corner Gate, and from the Tower of Hananel to the royal winepresses.

We are told the "whole land" will be like the Arabah which is a desert. This seems to refer to the devastation described by the seventh bowl. But then, we are told Jerusalem will remain in its place and in fact, be raised up.

> **Isaiah 2:2** (NIV) In the last days the mountain of the Lord's temple will be established as chief among the mountains; it will be raised above the hills, and all nations will stream to it.

This verse is repeated again in Micah 4:1. Mt. Zion will be raised as "chief" of the mountains. This seems to be the opposite of what had happened in the seventh bowl. As all mountains disappear, Mt. Zion becomes the greatest of all mountains - and to it all nations will come.

Ezekiel 20:40 (NIV) For on my holy mountain, the high mountain of Israel, declares the Sovereign LORD, there in the land the entire house of Israel will serve me, and there I will accept them...

The Restoration of Israel

The plan throughout the scriptures has been for Israel to be God's chosen people set apart for Him; for Israel to be a holy priesthood through which the world would be blessed. God's plan has not changed.

> **Jeremiah 31:10** Hear the word of the LORD, O ye nations, and declare it in the isles afar off, and say, He that scattered Israel will gather him, and keep him, as a shepherd doth his flock. **11** For the LORD hath redeemed Jacob, and ransomed him from the hand of him that was stronger than he. **12** Therefore they shall come and sing in the **height of Zion**, and shall flow together to the goodness of the LORD, for wheat, and for wine, and for oil, and for the young of the flock and of the herd: and their soul shall be as a watered garden; and they shall not sorrow any more at all (emphasis added).

In Daniel, we read a major reason for the 70th Week was the judgment of Israel. However, Isaiah records how Israel will come to truly rely on Jesus – "the Holy One of Israel" as their Messiah. Where they relied on the Antichrist and his covenant, they will now truly rely on the Lord.

> **Isaiah 10:20-22** (NIV) In that day the remnant of Israel, the survivors of the house of Jacob, will no longer rely on him who struck them down but will truly rely on the LORD, the Holy One of Israel. {**21**} A remnant will return, a remnant of Jacob will return to the Mighty

God. {**22**} Though your people, O Israel, be like the sand by the sea, only a remnant will return. Destruction has been decreed, overwhelming and righteous.

We also see Israel will be restored from all nations, so this will be a restoration of everyone "who is called by my name."

> **Isaiah 43:5-7** (NIV) "Do not be afraid, for I am with you; I will bring your children from the east and gather you from the west. {**6**} I will say to the north, 'Give them up!' and to the south, 'Do not hold them back.' Bring my sons from afar and my daughters from the ends of the earth-- {**7**} everyone who is called by my name, whom I created for my glory, whom I formed and made."

The prophet Micah records how Israel will suffer God's judgment, but they will not be forsaken by the Lord. God's purpose in judgment is redemption.

> **Micah 7:7** Therefore I will look unto the LORD; I will wait for the God of my salvation: my God will hear me. **8** Rejoice not against me, O mine enemy: when I fall, I shall arise; when I sit in darkness, the LORD shall be a light unto me. **9** I will bear the indignation of the LORD, because I have sinned against him, until he plead my cause, and execute judgment for me: he will bring me forth to the light, and I shall behold his righteousness.

Isaiah records how God will include "foreigners" into His covenant, and God calls His house "a house of prayer *for all nations.*" Furthermore, the Lord is recorded as gathering "others" besides who He has already gathered. All of these references seem to indicate God's people in His millennial kingdom will not be defined by nationality, but by their commitment to the Lord.

Isaiah 56:6-8 (NIV) And foreigners who bind themselves to the LORD to serve him, to love the name of the LORD, and to worship him, all who keep the Sabbath without desecrating it and who hold fast to my covenant-- {**7**} these I will bring to my holy mountain and give them joy in my house of prayer. Their burnt offerings and sacrifices will be accepted on my altar; for my house will be called a house of prayer for all nations. {**8**}The Sovereign LORD declares-- he who gathers the exiles of Israel: "I will gather still others to them besides those already gathered."

The conclusion is the restoration of Israel will not be confined to a national identity. Rather, Israel will become a people who are identified by the spiritual condition of their hearts. We must not confuse these survivors with the bride of Christ who have been raptured. The raptured saints will have immortal bodies, and they will never die. The "new" Israel will be the survivors of the 70th Week of Daniel who have chosen to follow Jesus. They will still have mortal bodies and will continue to live their lives into the millennial kingdom.

The Restoration of the Temple

God's plan ever since the Garden of Eden has been to dwell with man. The prophet Ezekiel records the realization of God's plan and even reveals there will be a specific place where Christ's throne will be located. In verse 7, one can almost understand the reason for all the judgment and suffering as God claims His people will never again defile His name.

Ezekiel 43:6-7 (NIV) While the man was standing beside me, I heard someone speaking to me from inside the temple. {**7**} He said: "Son of man, this is the place of my throne and the place for the soles of my feet. This is where I will live among the Israelites forever. The house of Israel will never again defile my holy name--neither they nor their kings--by their prostitution and the lifeless idols of their kings at their high places."

We are told in Zechariah Jesus, Himself, will build God's temple. We are told in verse 15 those who are far away will come and help in this re-building, but the prophetic message is Jesus will direct the building of the millennial temple. He will rule as King and intercede as priest. Never again will God's people have to choose between obeying their ruler and being faithful to God.

> **Zechariah 6:12** And speak unto him, saying, Thus speaketh the LORD of hosts, saying, Behold the man whose name is The BRANCH; and he shall grow up out of his place, and he shall build the temple of the LORD: **13** Even he shall build the temple of the LORD; and he shall bear the glory, and shall sit and rule upon his throne; and he shall be a priest upon his throne: and the counsel of peace shall be between them both.

Christ to Rule Over the Earth

At last what God has intended and man has longed for will come to pass. God will live with man. There will never again be a challenge of who will rule God's people.

> **Daniel 7:11,13-14** (NIV) "Then I continued to watch because of the boastful words the horn was speaking. I kept looking until the beast was slain and its body destroyed and thrown into the blazing fire... {**13**} In my vision at night I looked, and there before me was one like a son of man, coming with the clouds of heaven... He approached the Ancient of Days and was led into his presence.

{**14**}He was given authority, glory and sovereign power; all peoples, nations and men of every language worshiped him. His dominion is an everlasting dominion that will not pass away, and his kingdom is one that will never be destroyed."

As the 45 day reclamation period closes a new chapter in the existence of man will begin. Christ will rule the earth for 1,000 years. The prophet Isaiah describes the time of the millennial reign of Christ in incredible terms. Life spans will increase and peace will reign on the earth even in the animal kingdom. The Lord's presence is described as "before they call I will answer."

Isaiah 65:20 (NIV) "Never again will there be in it an infant who lives but a few days, or an old man who does not live out his years; he who dies at a hundred will be thought a mere youth; he who fails to reach a hundred will be considered accursed... **23** They will not toil in vain or bear children doomed to misfortune; for they will be a people blessed by the LORD, they and their descendants with them. **24** Before they call I will answer; while they are still speaking I will hear. **25** The wolf and the lamb will feed together, and the lion will eat straw like the ox, but dust will be the serpent's food. They will neither harm nor destroy on all my holy mountain," says the LORD.

---

[1] Van Kampen, 425-436., Adapted.

Chapter 6
The Rapture

The rapture is the great "catching away" of all those who have trusted Christ - living and dead. The word "rapture" is not found in scripture. It is from the Latin Vulgate (ancient Latin translation of the Bible) "rapere" which means to "catch up." 1 Thessalonians 4:15-18 is the classic passage describing the event we call the rapture.

> **1 Thess 4:15** For this we say unto you by the word of the Lord, that we which are alive and remain unto the coming of the Lord shall not prevent them which are asleep. **16** For the Lord himself shall descend from heaven with a shout, with the voice of the archangel, and with the trump of God: and the dead in Christ shall rise first: **17** Then we which are alive and remain shall be **caught up** together with them in the clouds, to meet the Lord in the air: and so shall we ever be with the Lord. **18** Wherefore comfort one another with these words (emphasis added).

The fact the saints will be raptured is clear in scripture and there has not been much debate about the rapture itself. However, the timing of the rapture has been hotly debated for centuries. So, the question is: "When will the rapture occur?"

Figure 10: The Rapture When?

91

There are three major views as to when the rapture will occur:

1. **Pre-Tribulation Rapture**
2. **Mid-Tribulation Rapture**
3. **Post-Tribulation Rapture**

Figure 11: Three Views of the Rapture

The Pre-Tribulation position is: the rapture will occur at the beginning of Daniel's 70th Week. In fact, those holding to this view see the rapture as initiating the 70th Week. The Mid-Tribulation position is the rapture will occur at the mid-point of the 70th Week when the Antichrist demands the world worship him. The Post-Tribulation position is: the rapture will occur at the end of the 70th Week. This position views the second coming as exactly that - the second coming, Jesus will return at the Battle of Armageddon and rapture His saints. Let us examine each of these views in greater detail in reverse order.

Post-Tribulation Rapture

According to the Post-Tribulation view, the rapture will happen at the Battle of Armageddon. All during the 70th Week, God's wrath will be poured out upon this world. The Rapture will occur somewhere around the time of the Battle of Armageddon. Jesus will return one time to rescue the godly and put an end to the wicked.

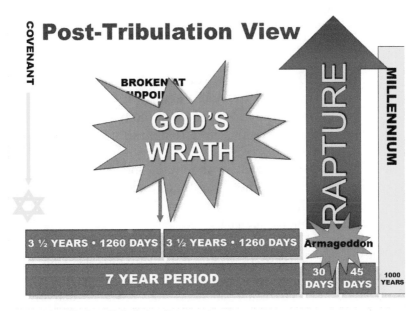

Figure 12: Post-Tribulation Rapture

There are some scriptural problems with this view. The first problem, according to this view, is God's people endure His wrath. There are those who argue God supernaturally protects His people during the outpouring of His wrath, but the scriptures seem to teach more than just protection.

> **Romans 5:9** (NIV) Since we have now been justified by his blood, how much more shall we be **saved from God's wrat**h through him! (emphasis added)

> **1 Thess 1:10** And to wait for his Son from heaven, whom he raised from the dead, even Jesus, **which delivered us from the wrath to come** (emphasis added).

1 Thess 5:9 For God hath **not appointed us to wrath**, but to obtain salvation by our Lord Jesus Christ (emphasis added)

Rev 3:10 (NIV) Since you have kept my command to endure patiently, I will also **keep you from the hour of trial** that is going to come upon the whole world to test those who live on the earth. (emphasis added)

Luke 21:36 Watch ye therefore, and pray always, that ye may be accounted worthy to **escape all these things that shall come to pass**, and to stand before the Son of man (emphasis added).

These are passages which indicate God has not just promised protection in the midst of His wrath, but an exemption from His wrath. The usage of the words "saved," "delivered," "not appointed," "keep you from" all seem to imply much more than God will protect you while His wrath is being poured upon the world.

There is another problem about the timing of the rapture. According to the scripture, no one knows the day or the hour when the rapture will occur - not even Jesus - only the Father. Now, if the rapture occurs at the Battle of Armageddon, then the day is predictable. Once the 70th Week begins, one must only wait 7 years plus 30 days.

Mark 13:32 But of that day and that hour knoweth no man, no, not the angels which are in heaven, neither the Son, but the Father.

A third problem is not one scripture clearly specifies this timing for the rapture. A fourth problem is a conflict in the timing of the Bema Judgment and the Marriage Supper of the Lamb which will follow the judgment. If God's saints are still on earth - how can they participate in the Bema Judgment or the Marriage Supper?

In addition, when would the judgment and marriage supper take place unless it happens after the millennial kingdom has begun.

A fifth problem is also a conflict in timing and is indicated in 1 Thessalonians 3:13.

> **1 Thessalonians 3:13** (NIV) May he strengthen your hearts so that you will be blameless and holy **in the presence of our God** and Father **when our Lord Jesus comes with all his holy ones**. (emphasis added)

If God's people are in His presence WHEN Jesus returns with His holy ones, then it is impossible for His people to be on the earth when Jesus returns! The resulting problems are...

- *God's people endure His wrath*

- *Predictability about the day and hour*

- *No scriptural basis for the timing of the rapture*

- *Conflict in timing of:*
  Bema Judgment
  Marriage Supper of the Lamb
  Saints in God's presence – cf.
  1 Thess 3:13

Mid-Tribulation Rapture

The Mid-Tribulation rapture position was actually a response to the problems created in the Post-Tribulation view. Because the scripture is so clear about God's people not enduring His wrath, some chose to see the rapture happening at the mid-point of the 70th Week. This position DID solve some of the problems. If the rapture occurred at the mid-point, then God's people would not suffer God's wrath, and the conflict in timing of the Bema Judgment and Marriage Supper of the Lamb are solved - as well as the conflict in 1 Thessalonians 3:13.

However, this position still did not solve the predictability problem. One must still only count 1,260 days after the beginning of the 70th Week. Also, there is no scriptural basis for the rapture occurring specifically at the mid-point of the 70th Week.

Pre-Tribulation Rapture

By far, the most popular view is the Pre-Tribulation position. This is what has been called the "left-behind" view. According to the Pre-Tribulation view, Jesus will rapture His people at the beginning of the 70th Week. God's people are completely absent from the earth during the entire 7 years except those who are saved during the 7 years.

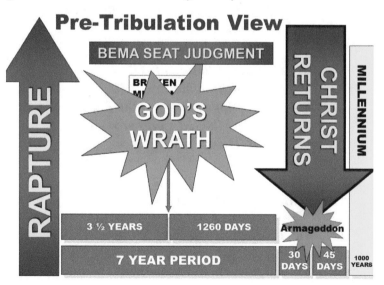

Figure 13: Pre-Tribulation Rapture

While the raptured saints are going through the Bema Judgment and the Marriage Supper of the Lamb; meanwhile, on earth, God's wrath is being poured out upon mankind. Many see God's people returning with Jesus at the Battle of Armageddon – see figure 13.

According to the Pre-Tribulation view, the Daniel's 70th Week is more commonly called "the tribulation period." This comes from Matthew 24 where the scripture records a time of tribulation such as never been seen before.

> **Matt 24:21** For then shall be great tribulation, such as was not since the beginning of the world to this time, no, nor ever shall be.

This view also separates the 70th Week into two halves calling the first 3 ½ years "The Tribulation" and the last 3 ½ years "The Great Tribulation."

This view teaches some very specific things are happening on the earth. There are three significant events specific to this view.

Figure 14:Events of Pre-Trib 7 Years

First, the seals, trumpets and bowls are all interpreted as signifying God's wrath, and they are poured out upon mankind during the entire 7 years. Second, the 144,000 Jews sealed in Revelation chapter seven are seen as Jewish evangelists who will usher in the greatest revival in history - which is the third significant event – see figure 14.

The idea of Jewish evangelists and the greatest revival come from the beginning of Revelation chapter 7.

> **Rev 7:3** Saying, Hurt not the earth, neither the sea, nor the trees, till we have sealed the servants of our God in their foreheads. 4 And I heard the number of them which were sealed: and there were sealed an hundred and forty and four thousand of all the tribes of the children of Israel. 5 Of the tribe of Juda were sealed twelve thousand. Of the tribe of Reuben were sealed twelve thousand. Of the tribe of Gad were sealed twelve thousand. 6 Of the tribe of Aser were sealed twelve thousand. Of the tribe of Nepthalim were sealed twelve thousand. Of the tribe of Manasses were sealed twelve thousand. 7 Of the tribe of Simeon were sealed twelve thousand. Of the tribe of Levi were sealed twelve thousand. Of the tribe of Issachar were sealed twelve thousand. 8 Of the tribe of Zabulon were sealed twelve thousand. Of the tribe of Joseph were sealed twelve thousand. Of the tribe of Benjamin were sealed twelve thousand. 9 After this I beheld, and, lo, a great multitude, which no man could number, of all nations, and kindreds, and people, and tongues, stood before the throne, and before the Lamb, clothed with white robes, and palms in their hands;

These evangelists and the revival explain the multitude that follow in verse 9; otherwise, there would be no way to account for this multitude that no one can count.

Unlike the Post-Tribulation view, the Pre-Tribulation has the proper scriptural balance between the deliverance of God's people and the punishment of the ungodly during the pouring out of the wrath of God.

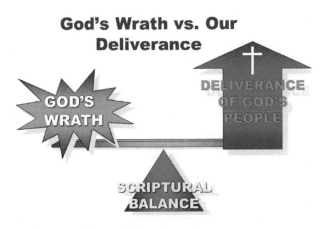

Figure 15: Scriptural Balance

The scripture declares God's wrath will punish the wicked, yet God's people will be "rescued from the coming wrath." This balance is depicted in figure 15.

The Pre-Tribulation view is the most popular view taught today and has been supported by popular books and movies. It is the view the majority of people has heard and believe. It is the view most often preached on television. It would be the most literal approach to prophecy and the most effective interpretation; however, it is weakened by the absence of scriptural support and by specific assumptions that have to be made in order to harmonize the scriptures.

Pre-Tribulation Assumptions

Webster's Dictionary defines an assumption as "supposing a thing without proof."[1] When it comes to theology, an assumption is a belief or doctrine not explicitly stated in scripture. Assumptions are made to explain why the scripture says what it says, rather than scripture explaining what we believe. Belief should be based on scripture and not scripture on belief.

There are six assumptions one must accept in order to adhere to a Pre-Tribulation Rapture view. Because of the logic of the Pre-Tribulation view, to reject these assumptions is to crumble the foundation of the view.

1. The 70th Week of Daniel is only for the Jewish Nation

The first assumption is the 70th Week of Daniel is only for the Jewish Nation: Israel and the church are separate entities and God cannot work with both at the same time. Many believe the Old Testament is for Jews only. It has been commonly stated when Jesus arose from the dead, the Jewish clock stopped and the Gentile clock started. When the 70th Week arrives, the Gentile clock will stop and the Jewish clock will start once again. This assumption is based on the scripture in Luke 21 among others.

> **Luke 21:23** But woe unto them that are with child, and to them that give suck, in those days! for there shall be great distress in the land, and wrath upon this people. 24 And they shall fall by the edge of the sword, and shall be led away captive into all nations: and Jerusalem shall be trodden down of the Gentiles, **until the times of the Gentiles be fulfilled** (emphasis added).

This is an assumption because this reasoning is not supported in scripture. For instance, on the day of Pentecost, the Apostle Peter spoke to the crowd and applied Old Testament prophecy to describe what was going on with the people who would become the new Christian church.

> **Acts 2:15** For these are not drunken, as ye suppose, seeing it is but the third hour of the day. 16 But this is that which was **spoken by the prophet Joel**; 17 And it shall come to pass in the last days, saith God, I will pour out of my Spirit upon all flesh: and your sons and your daughters shall prophesy, and your young men shall see visions, and your old men shall dream dreams: 18 And on my servants and on my handmaidens I will pour out in those days of my Spirit; and they shall prophesy: 19 And I will shew wonders in heaven above, and signs in the earth beneath; blood, and fire, and vapour of smoke: 20 The sun shall be turned into darkness, and the moon into blood, before that great and notable day of the Lord come: 21 And it shall come to pass, that whosoever shall call on the name of the Lord shall be saved (emphasis added).

Furthermore, he quotes the Old Testament prophecy regarding the Day of the Lord which should be an exclusively Jewish prophecy. The prophecy states: on that day everyone who calls "on the name of the Lord shall be saved" (Acts 2:20-21).

2. *Matthew 24 was written exclusively for the Jews*

The second assumption is Matthew chapter 24 was written exclusively for the Jews. This is an assumption because it is not explicitly stated in scripture, and it allows the reader to ignore this passage as irrelevant. We would not allow anyone to blatantly ignore any other passage in this same way.

The argument asserts Jesus was speaking to His disciples who were Jews about what would happen to the nation of Israel. Although, the disciples were Jewish, they were also "the church," and part of the Bride of Christ. As the Bride of Christ, these disciples would share the same experience as modern day Christians at Jesus' return.

Furthermore, even though they were Jewish, the scripture foretells the Jewish nation will reject Jesus as their Messiah. The Apostle Peter refuted the religious leaders of his day by quoting Old Testament scripture foretelling this.

> **Acts 4:10** (NIV) "then know this, you and all the people of Israel: It is by the name of Jesus Christ of Nazareth, whom you crucified but whom God raised from the dead, that this man stands before you healed. 11 **He is** `the stone you builders rejected, which has become the capstone.' 12 Salvation is found in no one else, for there is no other name under heaven given to men by which we must be saved." (emphasis added).

Matthew 24 includes statements that obviously include believers in Christ and, therefore, cannot apply to the Jews who would eventually reject Christ as their Messiah.

> **Matt 24:9** (NIV) "Then **you** will be handed over to be persecuted and put to death, and **you will be hated** by all nations **because of me**. 10 At that time many will **turn away from the faith** and will betray and hate each other (emphasis added)..."

Especially in the context of Christ's return, the focus of Matthew 24 being on the Jewish people would make no sense when it clearly emphasizes those who would be hated *because* of Jesus and those who would turn away from the faith.

3. Revelation 4:1 signifies the rapture

The third assumption is that Revelation 4:1 signifies the rapture.

> **Rev 4:1** After this I looked, and, behold, a door was opened in heaven: and the first voice which I heard was as it were of a trumpet talking with me; which said, Come up hither, and I will shew thee things which must be hereafter.

The Apostle John is exiled on the isle of Patmos, and Jesus appears to him in visions and instructs him to write down what he sees. In chapter four, John is told to "come up here" to heaven where his vision continues. Most that hold the Pre-Tribulation view see the words "come up here" as signifying the rapture - the catching away into heaven. The door is open in heaven, and the voice is like a trumpet.

The common themes of "going up to heaven" and the trumpet sound are there, however, this is what would be called circumstantial evidence. It is convenient because the timing for a pre-tribulation rapture is there, but this is a subjective reading of the scripture. The assumption that Rev. 4:1 describes the rapture has no real contextual evidence. The scripture does not indicate, in any way, this connection through the symbolism. The greatest weakness of the pre-tribulation view is a lack of scriptural support for the timing. This assumption becomes crucial for that reason.

4. The Holy Spirit is the Restrainer
cf. 2 Thess 2:7

In 2 Thessalonians 2:7, the "one who holds him back" is mentioned. In the New American Standard version of the Bible he is called the "restrainer." It is stated how someone holds back the Antichrist from being revealed until the proper time.

> **2 Thess 2:6-8** (NIV) And now you know what is holding him back, so that he may be revealed at the proper time. {7} For the secret power of lawlessness is already at work; but the **one who now holds it back** will continue to do so till **he is taken out of the way**. {8} And then the lawless one will be revealed, whom the Lord Jesus will overthrow with the breath of his mouth and destroy by the splendor of his coming. (emphasis added)

Those who hold to a Pre-Tribulation view adamantly insist that the "restrainer" is the Holy Spirit. Therefore, at the rapture He is taken out of the way with the church allowing the Antichrist to be revealed to the world. This, too, is an assumption because scripture does not identify this one "who holds back." However, the identification of the "restrainer" as the Holy Spirit adds emphasis to the church being absent along with the restrainer as the Antichrist is revealed.

5. 144,000 Jews sealed become evangelists

We have already mentioned the fifth assumption; it is the 144,000 Jews sealed in Revelation 7 become evangelists. This is an assumption because nowhere is this stated. The book of Revelation simply states they are sealed. There is not an indication, at this point, the 144,000 Jewish people are even saved. The implication of "sealing" would seem to be a protection because they are not redeemed. This assumption is closely connected to the next.

6. Greatest Revival in History during the 70ᵗʰ Week

The last assumption is: because of the Jewish evangelists, the greatest revival in history takes place during the 70th Week. This is an assumption because nowhere is there any indication that this revival takes place. It is assumed to explain the presence of the multitude that follows the sealing of these Jewish people.

> **Rev 7:9** After this I beheld, and, lo, a great multitude, which no man could number, of all nations, and kindreds, and people, and tongues, stood before the throne, and before the Lamb, clothed with white robes, and palms in their hands;

> **Rev 7:13** And one of the elders answered, saying unto me, What are these which are arrayed in white robes? and whence came they? 14 And I said unto him, Sir, thou knowest. And he said to me, These are they which came out of great tribulation, and have washed their robes, and made them white in the blood of the Lamb.

We stated under the last assumption there is no evidence that the 144,000 Jews were redeemed just sealed. In contrast, the vast multitude that appears in heaven are described as having washed their robes white in the blood of the Lamb. This is a picture of redemption.

Therefore, pre-tribulation adherents assume that the 144,000 Jews are the reason for the following multitude. On the contrary, during this time in the book of Revelation it is stressed that people were not willing to repent.

Rev 9:20 And the rest of the men which were not killed by these plagues yet repented not of the works of their hands, that they should not worship devils, and idols of gold, and silver, and brass, and stone, and of wood: which neither can see, nor hear, nor walk.

These last two assumptions regarding the 144,000 Jews and the great revival are important to validating a pre-tribulation perspective, because without them there is no explanation for the multitude that appears. If this multitude are raptured saints then the argument for a pre-tribulation rapture is destroyed.

Rejecting the Pre-Tribulation Assumptions

If one chooses to reject one of these assumptions, the pre-tribulation perspective begins to crumble. If we reject the assumption of the 70th Week being only for the Jewish nation, then we lose the reasoning for the rapture to happen before the "Tribulation Period." If God continues to deal with the Gentiles, then the emphasis for the church to be gone is lost. The point that the 70th Week is only for the Jews is impetus for the church to be raptured before the 70th Week of Daniel. Furthermore, the assumption of God dealing with the Jews and Gentiles separately is the foundation for much of the rest of the other five assumptions.

Another assumption is Matthew 24 only applies to the Jewish nation. If we dismiss that assumption, one is left to explain the "rapture event" described in verses 29-31. If this event is the rapture, it happens after the Abomination of Desolation which happens in the middle of the 70th Week. Therefore, either the rapture is not pre-tribulation, or there are two raptures.

Matt 24:29 Immediately after the tribulation of those days shall the sun be darkened, and the moon shall not give her light, and the stars shall fall from heaven, and the powers of the heavens shall be shaken: 30 And then shall appear the sign of the Son of man in heaven: and then shall all the tribes of the earth mourn, and they shall see the **Son of man coming in the clouds of heaven** with power and great glory. 31 And he shall **send his angels with a great sound of a trumpet**, and they shall **gather together his elect** from the four winds, from one end of heaven to the other (emphasis added).

If one rejects that Rev 4:1 signifies the rapture, then there is not a SINGLE scripture to support a rapture before the Tribulation Period. Rev 4:1 is the ONLY scripture used to explicitly support this timing.

To reject the 144,000 Jews sealed become evangelists, then there is no explanation of the "sealing," and no support for the following revival. And, if the revival is rejected then there is the impossible problem of explaining the vast multitude from every tribe, nation, and tongue appearing in heaven out of the Tribulation Period. Therefore, to have a Pre-Tribulation rapture view is to be locked into these six assumptions.

All of these assumptions make sense and build a pre-tribulation picture; however, they all require interpreting scripture beyond what the text says. Each assumption can be explained and reasoned; however, the number of assumptions causes questions, and promotes the conclusion this is a view that is forced to fit together.

Pre-Tribulation Problems

In addition to the assumptions, there are some scriptural problems with the Pre-Tribulation view. The first is that scripture mentions explicitly that the return of Christ will be unmistakable.

The Unmistakable Return of Christ

According to the Pre-Tribulation view, the rapture will be only known to those taken to heaven. The rest of the world will know only that multitudes have disappeared. However, scripture indicates on several occasions that when Christ returns it will be obvious.

> **Mat 24:26-27** (NIV) So if anyone tells you, 'There he is, out in the desert,' do not go out; or, 'Here he is, in the inner rooms,' do not believe it. {27} For as lightning that comes from the east is visible even in the west, so will be the coming of the Son of Man.

> **Luke 17:23-24** (NIV) Men will tell you, 'There he is!' or 'Here he is!' Do not go running off after them. {24} For the Son of Man in his day will be like the lightning, which flashes and lights up the sky from one end to the other.

> **Rev 1:7** (NIV) Look, he is coming with the clouds, and every eye will see him, even those who pierced him; and all the peoples of the earth will mourn because of him. So shall it be! Amen.

If the rapture is a "secret" to the world, how could these scriptures be relevant? Some have explained they are speaking of Jesus' return at the Battle of Armageddon. Even with that reasoning, why would Jesus make the distinction of not believing if someone tells you "there he is" or "here he is?" Also, the book of Revelation records the world seeing Jesus coming as early as chapter six right after the sixth seal is opened.

Revelation 6:15 And the kings of the earth, and the great men, and the rich men, and the chief captains, and the mighty men, and every bondman, and every free man, **hid themselves** in the dens and in the rocks of the mountains; 16 And said to the mountains and rocks, Fall on us, and **hide us** from the face of him that sitteth on the throne, and from the wrath of the Lamb (emphasis added).

Furthermore, why would Christ have not explicitly told his followers in the last day they would first be raptured, and then God's wrath would be poured upon the world? Why is the pre-tribulation rapture missing from end-time passages?

Absence of the Holy Spirit vs. Multitude Saved

Another problem is according to this view, the Holy Spirit will be absent from the world having been "taken out of the way" by the rapture of the church. Therefore, how do we explain the greatest revival in history and the great multitude saved when the Holy Spirit is no longer in the world? It has been argued the Holy Spirit will be present in the same way He was present in the Old Testament – on a mission by mission basis. And yet, a greater revival will take place than has ever happened in the history of the church.

Furthermore, scripture tells us rather than a multitude saved, God will cause those who reject Him to be deluded into delighting in wickedness.

2 Thess 2:10 ...them that perish; because they received not the love of the truth, that they might be saved. 11 And for this cause God shall send them strong delusion, that they should believe a lie: 12 That they all might be damned who believed not the truth, but had pleasure in unrighteousness.

As mentioned in the assumptions, we are also told in the book of Revelation that even after suffering God's wrath, people will still not repent.

Rev 9:20 And the rest of the men which were not killed by these plagues yet repented not of the works of their hands, that they should not worship devils, and idols of gold, and silver, and brass, and stone, and of wood: which neither can see, nor hear, nor walk (this is after the 6th trumpet has sounded)

Rather than a great revival taking place, it seems people will dive more into wickedness and rejecting God than ever before.

Matthew 24 Only for the Jews

Another problem is the application of Matthew 24 to the Jews only. The reasoning is as follows: Matthew 24 predicts persecution of God's people; therefore, it has to apply to Jews and converts during Tribulation Period. In addition, the Disciples were Jews and so He was speaking to them as Jews. However, the logic falls apart when one recognizes they were and are a part of the Bride of Christ – what would happen to them is the same as will happen to the church today! To dissect a section of scripture and to claim it has no relevance to the church is something that would not be allowed with any other passage of scripture! One cannot ignore what the scripture says because he doesn't like the message.

Two Raptures???

If there is a pre-tribulation rapture, then according to Matthew 24, there must be two raptures.

> **Matt 24:29** Immediately after the tribulation of those days shall the sun be darkened, and the moon shall not give her light, and the stars shall fall from heaven, and the powers of the heavens shall be shaken: 30 And then shall appear the sign of the Son of man in heaven: and then shall all the tribes of the earth mourn, and they shall see the Son of man coming in the clouds of heaven with power and great glory. 31 **And he shall send his angels with a great sound of a trumpet**, and they shall **gather together his elect** from the four winds, from one end of heaven to the other (emphasis added).

The Son of Man is in the clouds, there is a loud trumpet call, He sends his angels and gathers his elect. It sounds a lot like the rapture does it not? Therefore, if the rapture has already happened, there will be another very similar event - supposedly directed at the Jews.

What Comes First?

The scripture in 2 Thessalonians 2:3 also poses a problem.

> **2 Thess 2:1** Now we beseech you, brethren, by the coming of our Lord Jesus Christ, and by our gathering together unto him, …3 Let no man deceive you by any means: for that day shall not come, except there come a

falling away first, and that man of sin be revealed, the son of perdition;

This passage begins "concerning the coming of our Lord Jesus Christ and our being gathered to Him..." (NIV) Does this sound like he is speaking of the rapture? Then he goes on to say "that day" will not come until the "man of sin" (the Antichrist) is revealed. So, what comes first: the Antichrist or the rapture? According to the Apostle Paul, the "man of sin" must be revealed *before* we are gathered to Christ. This makes a pre-tribulation rapture impossible.

No Scriptural Evidence of Evangelists, Revival, or Pre-Tribulational Timing

Last, there is simply no scriptural evidence of Jewish evangelists, revivals, or for the timing of a pre-tribulation rapture. These are all assumptions and conjecture. On the contrary, the scripture indicates men will turn further away from God. Also, the only evidence of a pre-tribulation timing for the rapture is the convoluted interpretation of Rev 4:1, and passages which promise God's people will not endure His wrath.

Although, one could find implication of the pre-tribulation timing, explicit evidence is not there. Again, in addition to the assumptions, all of the Pre-Tribulation problems points can be argued, but the entire picture is still one where all the pieces seem to be forced to fit together! The question remains, "Is there a way to understand end-time prophecy where all the pieces just fall into place naturally?"

[1] Webster Dictionary, http://www.webster-dictionary.net/definition/assumption/ (accessed January 18, 2013).

Chapter 7
The Day of the Lord

In the last chapter we examined the event in scripture commonly called "the rapture." It is described in 1 Thessalonians 4:15-18 as being the event when all the saints of God, living and dead, will be gathered to meet Jesus in the air, and be taken home to heaven. We examined how the actual timing of the rapture has been debated for ages, and that there are three views that are the most prominent. We investigated each in detail.

Pre-Tribulation Rapture

Mid-Tribulation Rapture

Post-Tribulation Rapture

After analyzing each position, it became obvious that each view has its problems and none seem to fit all of scripture in a natural way. So, we ended up with the question, "is there a way to understand end-time prophecy where all the pieces just fall into place naturally?"

The whole purpose of this study is to provide the answer "**YES!**" But, to understand the rapture and the issues surrounding the timing, we must first understand what the Bible teaches about the Day of the Lord. So, we will now examine what the scripture teaches and discover what "The Day of the Lord" is.

GIt is surprising to find there is a great deal of information in the Bible regarding The Day of the Lord. Yet, I have heard very little preaching on the topic. Some have tried to interpret different meanings to the few times when the Day of Christ is mentioned, and there are many general references like "that day." This study interprets all of these references to the same event.

The Day of the Lord in the Old Testament

For the next few pages we will introduce many scriptures regarding the Day of the Lord and what the Bible has to say about that day.

A Day of Wrath on the Unrighteous

In the Old Testament, the Day of the Lord is described as a day of wrath and judgment on the unrighteous.

> **Isaiah 13:6** Howl ye; for the day of the LORD is at hand; it shall come as a destruction from the Almighty. 7 Therefore shall all hands be faint, and every man's heart shall melt: 8 And they shall be afraid: pangs and sorrows shall take hold of them; they shall be in pain as a woman that travaileth: they shall be amazed one at another; their faces shall be as flames. 9 Behold, the day of the LORD cometh, cruel both with wrath and fierce anger, to lay the land desolate: and he shall destroy the sinners thereof out of it.

Isaiah continues...

> **Isaiah 13:11** And I will punish the world for their evil, and the wicked for their iniquity; and I will cause the

arrogancy of the proud to cease, and will lay low the haughtiness of the terrible. ...13 Therefore I will shake the heavens, and the earth shall remove out of her place, in the wrath of the LORD of hosts, and in the day of his fierce anger.

A Division of the Real from the Religious

The Day of the Lord is also a dividing of the religious vs. those who "truly rely on the Lord"

> **Amos 8:3** And the songs of the temple shall be howlings in that day, saith the Lord GOD: there shall be many dead bodies in every place; they shall cast them forth with silence. 4 Hear this, O ye that swallow up the needy, even to make the poor of the land to fail, 5 Saying, When will the new moon be gone, that we may sell corn? and the sabbath, that we may set forth wheat, making the ephah small, and the shekel great, and falsifying the balances by deceit?

This verse described people who are religious. They are singing in the temple and they observe the Sabbath; however, their heart is in their pocketbooks. Although they are religious, they have no problem cheating to make a few extra bucks. It seems they practice the modern day separation of church and state.

Day of Judgment on Israel

Daniel depicts the 70th Week as a time for God to deal with the nation Israel. He describes it as applying to the nation and their holy city. There is no question that the 70th Week has been decreed for the nation of Israel. However, opposed to the pre-tribulation view, it is not for Israel exclusively.

> **Daniel 9:24** Seventy weeks are determined upon thy people and upon thy holy city...

Jeremiah describes God's judgment on all nations and also reserved for Israel.

> **Jeremiah 30:11** For I am with thee, saith the LORD, to save thee: though I make a full end of all nations whither I have scattered thee, yet will I not make a full end of thee: but I will correct thee in measure, and will not leave thee altogether unpunished.

The next verse describes those of Israel who have become complacent and tired of waiting on God. They feel God will do nothing about their sinful condition.

> **Zephaniah 1:11-12** (NIV) Wail, you who live in the market district ; all your merchants will be wiped out, all who trade with silver will be ruined. {12} At that time I will search Jerusalem with lamps and punish those who are complacent, who are like wine left on its dregs, who think, 'The LORD will do nothing, either good or bad.'

But, the Day of the Lord will be dire judgment. These passages reflect the intensity and unexpected impact that God's judgment will have upon the world.

> **Zeph 1:17** And I will bring distress upon men, that they shall walk like blind men, because they have sinned against the LORD: and their blood shall be poured out as dust, and their flesh as the dung. 18 Neither their silver nor their gold shall be able to deliver them in the day of the LORD'S wrath; but the whole land shall be

devoured by the fire of his jealousy: for he shall make even a speedy riddance of all them that dwell in the land.

Amos 5:18 Woe unto you that desire the day of the LORD! to what end is it for you? the day of the LORD is darkness, and not light. 19 As if a man did flee from a lion, and a bear met him; or went into the house, and leaned his hand on the wall, and a serpent bit him.

Jeremiah 4:10 (NIV) Then I said, "Ah, Sovereign LORD, how completely you have deceived this people and Jerusalem by saying, 'You will have peace,' when the sword is at our throats."

Aliens will be joined to Israel

In connection with the Day of the Lord there are several references of God's deliverance for Israel and also for non-Israelites. Israel is said to trust the Holy One and be joined by aliens or strangers as God's people.

Isaiah 10:20 (NIV) In that day the remnant of Israel, the survivors of the house of Jacob, will no longer rely on him who struck them down but will truly rely on the LORD, the Holy One of Israel.

Isaiah 14:1 For the LORD will have mercy on Jacob, and will yet choose Israel, and set them in their own land: and the strangers shall be joined with them, and they shall cleave to the house of Jacob.

God purifies His people

In addition to the judgment and deliverance of Israel, The Day of the Lord is also described as a time for God to purify His people. It is amazing that even in the midst of judgment God's objective is redemption.

> **Zephaniah 2:1** Gather yourselves together, yea, gather together, O nation not desired; 2 Before the decree bring forth, before the day pass as the chaff, before the fierce anger of the LORD come upon you, before the day of the LORD'S anger come upon you. 3 Seek ye the LORD, all ye meek of the earth, which have wrought his judgment; seek righteousness, seek meekness: it may be ye shall be hid in the day of the LORD'S anger.

> **Zephaniah 3:8-9** (NIV) "Therefore wait for me," declares the LORD, "for the day I will stand up to testify. I have decided to assemble the nations, to gather the kingdoms and to pour out my wrath on them-- all my fierce anger. The whole world will be consumed by the fire of my jealous anger. {9} Then will I purify the lips of the peoples, that all of them may call on the name of the LORD and serve him shoulder to shoulder."

A day when He comes to live among His people

It is incredible that in the midst of judgment concerning the Day of the Lord, it is also mentioned as a fulfillment of God's plan to dwell with His people.

Zechariah 2:10-11 (NIV) "Shout and be glad, O Daughter of Zion. For I am coming, and I will live among you," declares the LORD. {11} "Many nations will be joined with the LORD in that day and will become my people. I will live among you and you will know that the LORD Almighty has sent me to you."

Day of wrath like never before or ever again

There is also the description of the Day of the Lord as being worse than anything happening in all of history.

Joel 2:1 Blow ye the trumpet in Zion, and sound an alarm in my holy mountain: let all the inhabitants of the land tremble: for the day of the LORD cometh, for it is nigh at hand; 2 A day of darkness and of gloominess, a day of clouds and of thick darkness, as the morning spread upon the mountains: a great people and a strong; there hath not been ever the like, neither shall be any more after it, even to the years of many generations.

Last call to return to the Lord

In Joel is an incredible passage again recounting God's mercy in the midst of His judgment. Even while His wrath is being poured out the Lord says, "Even now... return to me with all your heart." God's judgment is designed to bring about repentance.

Joel 2:10-13 (NIV) Before them the earth shakes, the sky trembles, the sun and moon are darkened, and the stars no longer shine. {11} The LORD thunders at the head of his army; his forces are beyond number, and mighty are those who obey his command. The day of the LORD is great; it is dreadful. Who can endure it? {12} **'Even now,'** declares the LORD, **'return to me with all your heart**, with fasting and weeping and mourning.' {13} Rend your heart and not your garments. Return to the LORD your God, for he is gracious and compassionate, slow to anger and abounding in love, and he relents from sending calamity (emphasis added).

A Day of Deliverance

In addition to the deliverance of Israel, the Day of the Lord is said to be deliverance for "everyone who calls on the name of the Lord"

> **Joel 2:31-32** (NIV) The sun will be turned to darkness and the moon to blood before the coming of the great and dreadful day of the LORD. {32} And everyone who calls on the name of the LORD will be saved; for on Mount Zion and in Jerusalem there will be deliverance...

The Sign of the Day of the Lord

One of the most important aspects of the Day of the Lord that is found throughout the scriptures is the Sign of the Day of the Lord: sun and stars darkened, moon darkened to blood. This is an explicit sign mentioned numerous times that will precede the Day of the Lord.

Joel 2:10 The earth shall quake before them; the heavens shall tremble: the sun and the moon shall be dark, and the stars shall withdraw their shining:

Joel 2:31 The sun shall be turned into darkness, and the moon into blood, before the great and the terrible day of the LORD come.

Joel 3:14 Multitudes, multitudes in the valley of decision: for the day of the LORD is near in the valley of decision. 15 The sun and the moon shall be darkened, and the stars shall withdraw their shining.

Amos 8:9 And it shall come to pass in that day, saith the Lord GOD, that I will cause the sun to go down at noon, and I will darken the earth in the clear day:

We can divide these Old Testament verses into three major themes surrounding the prophecies regarding the Day of the Lord. First, there is a sign of the Day of the Lord. The sun is darkened and the moon turns to blood (red) and the stars no longer shine. Second, God is coming to judge Israel and the world for their sin. And, third, there is a theme of deliverance: "Rend your hearts and not your garments," "return to the Lord your God," "Everyone who calls upon the name of the Lord will be saved."

The Sign of the Day of the Lord

Judgment for Sin

Deliverance for God's People

The Day of the Lord in the New Testament

The Day of the Lord is definitely a theme throughout the Old Testament. Is it mentioned in the New Testament?

> **Matt 24:29** Immediately after the tribulation of those days shall the **sun be darkened, and the moon shall not give her light, and the stars shall fall from heaven**, and the powers of the heavens shall be shaken: 30 And then shall appear the sign of the Son of man in heaven: and then shall all the tribes of the earth mourn, and they shall see the Son of man coming in the clouds of heaven with power and great glory. 31 And he shall send his angels with a great sound of a trumpet, and they shall gather together his elect from the four winds, from one end of heaven to the other (emphasis added).

> **Mark 13:24** But in those days, after that tribulation, the **sun shall be darkened, and the moon shall not give her light, 25 And the stars of heaven shall fall**, and the powers that are in heaven shall be shaken. 26 And then shall they see the Son of man coming in the clouds with great power and glory. 27 And then shall he send his angels, and shall gather together his elect from the four winds, from the uttermost part of the earth to the uttermost part of heaven (emphasis added).

> **Luke 21:25** And there shall be **signs in the sun, and in the moon, and in the stars**; and upon the earth distress of nations, with perplexity; the sea and the waves roaring; 26 Men's hearts failing them for fear, and for looking after those things which are coming on the earth: for the powers of heaven shall be shaken. 27 And then shall they see the Son of man coming in a cloud with power and great glory. 28 And when these things begin to come to pass, then look up, and lift up your

heads; for your redemption draweth nigh (emphasis added).

Acts 2:20 The sun shall be turned into darkness, and the moon into blood, before that great and notable **day of the Lord** come: 21 And it shall come to pass, that whosoever shall call on the name of the Lord shall be saved (emphasis added).

Three Themes in the New Testament

There are three themes present in the scriptures from the New Testament concerning the Day of the Lord.

The Sign of the Day of the Lord

Jesus comes in Power and Glory

Salvation/Deliverance

They are: the sign of sun, moon, and stars just before Jesus comes in power and great glory, and there is a theme of salvation and deliverance: "gather His elect," "Redemption is drawing near," "everyone who calls… will be saved."

Based on these observations, is the Day of the Lord mentioned in the book of Revelation, and are these three themes present?

The Day of the Lord in the Book of Revelation

The most explicit passage in the book of Revelation which applies to the Day of the Lord is found in chapters six and seven.

Rev 6:12 And I beheld when he had opened the sixth seal, and, lo, there was a great earthquake; and the **sun became black as sackcloth of hair, and the moon became as blood**; 13 And the stars of heaven fell unto the earth, even as a fig tree casteth her untimely figs, when she is shaken of a mighty wind. 14 And the heaven departed as a scroll when it is rolled together; and every mountain and island were moved out of their places. 15 And the kings of the earth, and the great men, and the rich men, and the chief captains, and the mighty men, and every bondman, and every free man, hid themselves in the dens and in the rocks of the mountains; 16 And said to the mountains and rocks, Fall on us, and hide us from the face of him that sitteth on the throne, and from the wrath of the Lamb: 17 For the **great day of his wrath is come**; and who shall be able to stand? (emphasis added)

Rev 7:3 Saying, Hurt not the earth, neither the sea, nor the trees, till we have sealed the servants of our God in their foreheads. 4 And I heard the number of them which were sealed: and there were sealed an hundred and forty and four thousand of all the tribes of the children of Israel.

Rev 7:9 After this I beheld, and, lo, a great multitude, which no man could number, of all nations, and kindreds, and people, and tongues, stood before the throne, and before the Lamb, clothed with white robes, and palms in their hands; 10 And cried with a loud voice, saying, **Salvation to our God** which sitteth upon the throne, and unto the Lamb (emphasis added).

Rev 7:13 And one of the elders answered, saying unto me, What are these which are arrayed in white robes? and whence came they? 14 And I said unto him, Sir, thou knowest. And he said to me, These are they which came out of great tribulation, and have **washed their robes**, and made them white **in the blood of the Lamb** (emphasis added).

Again, the themes of the sign of the Day of the Lord, Jesus coming in power and glory, and salvation and deliverance for God's people are present. It becomes overwhelming that the doctrine of the Day of the Lord was known in the Old and New Testaments and taught in the book of Revelation. Now, another question remains...

What About the Rapture?

In 2 Thessalonians 2 Paul writes about the "coming of our Lord Jesus Christ" and "our being gathered to Him." Now, what is this event? These two descriptions describing a single event can only point to the rapture of the saints. Then in verse 2, he names the event that is described as the "coming" and "gathering" and calls it "the Day of the Lord."...

> **2 Thess 2:1** (NIV) Concerning the coming of our Lord Jesus Christ and our being gathered to him, we ask you, brothers, 2 not to become easily unsettled or alarmed by some prophecy, report or letter supposed to have come from us, saying that the **day of the Lord** has already come (emphasis added).

The major passage dealing with the rapture is in 1 Thessalonians 4:17-18. The consensus of opinion is this passage provides the details about the rapture of the saints.

> **1 Thess 4:17** (NIV) After that, we who are still alive and are left will be caught up together with them in the clouds to meet the Lord in the air. And so we will be

with the Lord forever. 18 Therefore encourage each other with these words.

It is important to remember, though, that in the original language there were no chapter divisions. So, the Apostle Paul writes about the rapture and then continues in chapter 5 verse 1 immediately...

> **1 Thess 5:1** (NIV) Now, brothers, about times and dates we do not need to write to you, 2 for you know very well that the **day of the Lord** will come like a thief in the night (emphasis added).

The Apostle Paul has just been telling them what it will be like when Jesus returns to rapture the church, and immediately he begins to address when this will happen. It is blatantly obvious what he has been talking about, he calls "the Day of the Lord." The realization that the Bible DOES talk about the rapture, but the Biblical term for the rapture IS "the Day of the Lord" is a stark revelation. Now, we must ask, "Have we missed the fact that the 'Day of the Lord' and 'The Rapture' are the same event?"

Chapter 8
The "PreWrath" Rapture

As we consider the Rapture or The Day of the Lord, there is a comparison that Jesus made on several occasions. As Jesus taught His disciples, He compared His return to the days of Noah and Lot.

Noah and Lot

> **Luke 17:26-27** (NIV) Just as it was in the days of Noah, so also will it be in the days of the Son of Man. {27} People were eating, drinking, marrying and being given in marriage **up to the day** Noah entered the ark. **Then the flood came** and destroyed them all. (emphasis added)

This same thought is repeated in Matthew...

> **Matt 24:37-39** (NIV) As it was in the days of Noah, so it will be at the coming of the Son of Man. {38} For in the days before the flood, people were eating and drinking, marrying and giving in marriage, **up to the day** Noah entered the ark; {39} and they knew nothing about what would happen **until the flood came** and took them all away. That is how it will be at the coming of the Son of Man. (emphasis added)

There have been many sermons on Noah and Lot, but the idea usually conveyed is: the world was going on just as it always had until judgment came - people were eating, drinking, marrying and giving in marriage right up until the flood came. The thought most often preached is the unexpected nature of

Christ's return; however, this is not what this passage is teaching.

The idea the passage is teaching was judgment and deliverance came on a single day. This becomes even more apparent when we look back at the Genesis story.

> **Gen 7:1-4** (NIV) The LORD then said to Noah, "Go into the ark, you and your whole family, because I have found you righteous in this generation. {2} Take with you seven... {4} **Seven days from now** I will send rain on the earth for forty days and forty nights, and I will wipe from the face of the earth every living creature I have made." (emphasis added)

In Genesis, God begins by telling Noah in seven days the judgment flood will come. Many have used this verse to support a Pre-Tribulation view which is just as God warned Noah the flood would come in seven days, the rapture will happen at the beginning of the seven years. The problem is the story does not unfold that way. For, we are told a few verses later in the story...

> **Gen 7:12-13** (NIV) And rain fell on the earth forty days and forty nights. {13} **On that very day** Noah and his sons, Shem, Ham and Japheth, together with his wife and the wives of his three sons, entered the ark. (emphasis added)

Here in Genesis a few verses later, we are told precisely that the rain fell on the earth on the exact day that Noah and his family entered the ark. In fact, it is almost as if the narrator of this story wants to make sure we do not miss this by using the words, "on that very day."

Now, back to Luke 17, the same illustration continues and includes Lot.

Luke 17:29-35 (NIV) **But the day** Lot left Sodom, fire and sulfur rained down from heaven and destroyed them all. {30} **"It will be just like this on the day** the Son of Man is revealed. {31}On that day no one who is on the roof of his house, with his goods inside, should go down to get them. Likewise, no one in the field should go back for anything. {32} **Remember Lot's wife!** {33} Whoever tries to keep his life will lose it, and whoever loses his life will preserve it. {34} I tell you, on that night two people will be in one bed; one will be taken and the other left. {35} Two women will be grinding grain together; one will be taken and the other left" (emphasis added).

Again, with Lot, the scripture seems adamant to point out the exact day Lot left Sodom the judgment of God fell. Note in Luke 17:30, the writer states, "It will be just like this on the day the Son of Man is revealed." So, rather than teaching the unexpected nature of Christ's return, these passages are graphically depicting the Day of the Lord. The message of these passages is that on the day God's people are delivered, sudden judgment will come. A single day contains the turning point containing God's deliverance of His people and His judgment on the world.

On a single day:

- Noah and his family were delivered
- God wrath was poured out in the form of the flood
- Lot left Sodom
- God's wrath rained down in fire and sulphur

On a single day, in both cases, God delivered His people while pouring judgment out on the wicked. Luke 17 makes an amazing statement comparing this to Jesus' return...

"It will be just like this on the day the Son of Man is revealed."

Luke 17:30 (NIV)

So, when Jesus is revealed at His return, on a single day God's people will be delivered and judgment will be poured out on the wicked. This describes the Day of the Lord. On a single day God will rapture His people and will initiate the Day of the Lord when God will pour out His wrath upon this world. Combining the teaching about the Day of the Lord and the Rapture is what made all the prophecies begin to fall together naturally and make sense. This view is called...

The Pre-Wrath Rapture

2 Pet 2:5-7,9 (NIV) if he did not spare the ancient world when he brought the flood on its ungodly people, but **protected Noah**, a preacher of righteousness, and seven others; {6} if he condemned the cities of Sodom and Gomorrah by burning them to ashes, and made them an example of what is going to happen to the ungodly; {7} and if he **rescued Lot**, a righteous man, who was distressed by the filthy lives of lawless men {9} if this is so, then the Lord **knows how to rescue godly men** from trials and to **hold the unrighteous for the day of judgment**, while continuing their punishment (emphasis added).

The gospels contain this comparison of Noah and Lot, and indicate that God's deliverance (the Rapture) and His judgment (wrath) will happen or commence on a single day. Do we find this concept in other prophetic books like the book of Revelation?

Does the book of Revelation support the Pre-Wrath view of the end-times?

Rev 6:12 And I beheld when he had opened the sixth seal, and, lo, there was a great earthquake; and **the sun became black as sackcloth of hair, and the moon became as blood**; 13 And the stars of heaven fell unto the earth, even as a fig tree casteth her untimely figs, when she is shaken of a mighty wind. 14 And the heaven departed as a scroll when it is rolled together; and every mountain and island were moved out of their places. 15 And the kings of the earth, and the great men, and the rich men, and the chief captains, and the mighty men, and every bondman, and every free man, hid themselves in the dens and in the rocks of the mountains; 16 And said to the mountains and rocks, Fall on us, and hide us from the face of him that sitteth on the throne, and from the **wrath of the Lamb: 17 For the great day of his wrath is come; and who shall be able to stand?** (emphasis added)

Rev 7:9 After this I beheld, and, lo, a **great multitude, which no man could number**, of all nations, and kindreds, and people, and tongues, stood before the throne, and before the Lamb, clothed with white robes, and **palms in their hands**; 10 And cried with a loud voice, saying, Salvation to our God which sitteth upon the throne, and unto the Lamb.

In the book of Revelation, we are explicitly told this sign of the sun, moon and stars signals the day of the wrath of the Lamb. Immediately after the day of wrath begins, we find this multitude in heaven no one can count from every tribe and nation. It is interesting they are wearing robes and have palm branches in their hands; therefore, they must have resurrected bodies. Furthermore, we are told in Revelation, these are people having robes washed in the blood of the Lamb.

> **Revelation 7:14** ...These are they which came out of great tribulation, and have washed their robes, and made them white in the blood of the Lamb.

This is a multitude no one can count, they are from every nation and tongue on earth, and they are people whose sins have been washed by the blood of the Lamb. Who else could this multitude be except the raptured saints from all the ages!

Now, there is one other point to consider as we look at Noah. Many have puzzled over the passage regarding Noah and Lot in the book of Matthew when considering the word "taken" and "took." The scripture seems to indicate the people in the field and grinding at the mill "taken" is a reference to the rapture. Some have questioned since those "taken" in the flood were the ungodly and were destroyed; are the ones "taken" while in the field or grinding at the mill to be considered the ungodly also which are destroyed? If so, this undermines the idea of this passage being a reference to the rapture. It creates a new dilemma interpreting this passage especially since the scripture declares "this is how it will be at the coming of the Son of Man."

Matthew 24:39-41 (NIV) and they knew nothing about what would happen until the flood came and **took** them all away. That is how it will be at the coming of the Son of Man. {40} Two men will be in the field; one will be **taken** and the other left. {41} Two women will be grinding with a hand mill; one will be **taken** and the other left (emphasis added).

This passage does seem to raise the question as to the reference to those "taken." What is the connection between those "taken" in the flood and those "taken" at the coming of the Son of man. Some have speculated since those in the flood were taken to destruction, it is those "left" who will meet the Lord. However, what we don't see is there are two different verbs in the original language. For those taken in the flood the verb is "airo" (figure 16), which means "to take away" or "remove."[1]

Dictionary entry:

αἴρω

take, take up;
take away, remove
set aside Col 2:14); *carry; sweep away* (of a flood); *raise* (of one's voice); *take over, conquer* (Jn 11:48); *kill* (Jn 19:15); *keep in suspense* (Jn 10:24)

Figure 16: airo

The second verb is different. It is the word "paralambano" (figure 17) which means "to take along," "receive," or "accept."[2] Therefore this verse is saying those "taken" in the flood were "removed" while those "taken" at the coming of the

Son of man were "received." Therefore, this illustration of what will happen "at the coming of the Son of Man" does apply to the rapture of God's people.

Dictionary entry:

παραλαμβάνω

take, take along; receive, accept

(often of a tradition); *learn* (1 Th 4:1); *take charge of* (Jn 19:16b)

Figure 17: paralambano

What becomes apparent is the real message of the passage is not the comparison about the ones "taken." The real message is the comparison of unexpected judgment and redemption at the same time – in fact, the same day.

Once the Day of the Lord begins – two things will happen: God's people will be rescued and then judgment begins. Just as the flood and fire destroyed those who rejected God, the Day of the Lord's wrath will fall on the world that has rejected Christ. However, God's people will not be facing judgment; they will be delivered.

> **Matt 24:36-39** (NIV) **No one knows** about that day or hour, not even the angels in heaven, nor the Son, but only the Father. {37} As it was in the days of Noah, so it will be at the coming of the Son of Man. {39} ...**and they knew nothing** about what would happen until the flood came and took them all away. **That is how it will be at the coming of the Son of Man.** (emphasis added)

The scripture is clear that no one knows when this particular day will be, but when the appointed day arrives God's people will be raptured and God's wrath will begin to be poured out upon the world. 2 Thessalonians 1:4-10 describe how God's plan has been to rescue the godly while bringing punishment upon those who have rejected Him.

> **2 Thess 1:4-10** (NIV) Therefore, among God's churches we boast about your perseverance and faith in all the persecutions and trials you are enduring. {5} All this is evidence that God's judgment is right, and **as a result you will be counted worthy of the kingdom of God**, for which you are suffering. {6} God is just: He will pay back trouble to those who trouble you {7} and **give relief** to you who are troubled, and to us as well. **This will happen when** the Lord Jesus is revealed from heaven in blazing fire with his powerful angels. {8} He will punish those who do not know God and do not obey the gospel of our Lord Jesus. {9} They will be punished with everlasting destruction and shut out from the presence of the Lord and from the majesty of his power {10} **on the day** he comes **to be glorified in his holy people** and to be marveled at among all those who have believed. **This includes you**, because you believed our testimony to you. (emphasis added)

---

[1] Barclay M. Newman, *A Concise Greek-English Dictionary of the New Testament* (London: United Bible Societies, 1971), 5.

[2] Ibid., 133.

Chapter 9
The Timing of the Rapture

We have uncovered the Pre-Wrath view of the rapture, and looked at validating the Pre-Wrath view by harmonizing the prophecies concerning Noah and Lot. The next task is to determine the timing of the rapture according to what the scripture teaches. The Bible tells us there are three events that will happen together at the Day of the Lord.

The Sign of the Day of the Lord

Jesus comes in Power and Glory

Salvation/Deliverance

So, in order to determine the timing, we must look for these events in prophecy and discern if there is consistency as to the time when these things will occur. The book of Revelation locates the sign of the Day of the Lord after the sixth seal is broken.

> **Rev 6:12** And I beheld when he had opened the **sixth seal**, and, lo, there was a great earthquake; and the **sun became black** as sackcloth of hair, and the **moon became as blood**; 13 And the **stars of heaven fell unto the earth**, even as a fig tree casteth her untimely figs, when she is shaken of a mighty wind (emphasis added).

Now, we must determine what are these seals, and what do they signify. In the prior chapter of Revelation, we are told of a scroll sealed with seven seals. These seals were common in the Apostle John's day. A scroll could be sealed with multiple seals, but it could not be opened until all the seals had been broken.

> **Rev 5:1-2** (NIV) Then I saw in the right hand of him who sat on the throne a scroll with writing on both sides and **sealed with seven seals**. {2} And I saw a mighty angel proclaiming in a loud voice, "Who is worthy to **break the seals** and **open the scroll?**" (emphasis added)

Figure 18: The 7 Sealed Scroll

The scroll is sealed with seven seals and as the sixth seal is broken the sign of the Day of the Lord takes place. When the seventh seal is broken the scroll is opened and the Day of the Lord's wrath begins. Therefore, we can surmise the scroll sealed with seven seals IS the scroll of the "Day of the Lord."

The sequence of events as the sixth seal is broken follows what we have seen as the events surrounding the Day of the Lord.

Rev 6:12 And I beheld when he had opened the sixth seal, and, lo, there was a great earthquake; and the **sun became black** as sackcloth of hair, and the moon became as blood; 13 And the stars of heaven fell unto the earth, even as a fig tree casteth her untimely figs, when she is shaken of a mighty wind (emphasis added).

The Sign of the Day of the Lord

Rev 6:16 And said to the mountains and rocks, Fall on us, and **hide us from the face of him** that sitteth on the throne, and from the wrath of the Lamb: 17 For the great day of his wrath is come; and who shall be able to stand? (emphasis added)

Jesus comes in power and glory

Rev 7:9 After this I beheld, and, lo, a great multitude, which no man could number, of all nations, and kindreds, and people, and tongues, stood before the throne, and before the Lamb, clothed with white robes, and palms in their hands; 10 And cried with a loud voice, saying, Salvation to our God which sitteth upon the throne, and unto the Lamb.

The Rapture – Salvation/Deliverance

So, based on the scripture in the book of Revelation, we can conclude the rapture will follow the breaking of the sixth seal before the Day of the Lord's wrath begins.

The Seven Seals of Revelation

> **Rev 6:1-2** (NIV) I watched as the Lamb opened the **first of the seven seals**. Then I heard one of the four living creatures say in a voice like thunder, "Come!" {2} I looked, and there before me was a white horse! Its rider held a bow, and **he was given a crown**, and he rode out **as** a conqueror bent on conquest. (emphasis added)

The rider on a white horse looks and sounds like a hero; however, the implication is he does not deserve his title. He was given a crown which seems to indicate it was not earned. Secondly, we are told he rode out as a conqueror. Most scholars agree this seal describes the appearance of the Antichrist on the scene. He will begin the 70th Week by looking like the answer to the problems of the world. The first half of the 70th Week will be a time of maneuvering and posturing by the Antichrist to consolidate his power.

> **Rev 6:3** And when he had opened the **second seal**, I heard the second beast say, Come and see. 4 And there went out another horse that was red: and **power was given to him that sat thereon to take peace from the earth**, and that they should kill one another: and there was given unto him a great sword (emphasis added).

The second seal is a rider on a fiery red horse, and its rider was given power to take peace from the earth. This seal symbolizes war. This seal could symbolize the Antichrist using military power to continue his rise to worldwide power.

> **Rev 6:5-6** (NIV) When the Lamb opened the **third seal**... I looked, and there before me was a black horse! Its rider was holding a pair of scales in his hand. {6} Then I heard... "**A quart of wheat for a day's wages**, and three quarts of barley for a day's wages, and do not damage the oil and the wine!" (emphasis added)

The third seal is a rider on a black horse and we are told a quart of wheat will sell for a day's wages. This is a reference to the coming of famine. When war and famine strike, people are more willing to accept someone who can provide for their needs. By the time of the third and fourth seal we should be approaching the Abomination of Desolation.

> **Rev 6:7** And when he had opened the **fourth seal**, I heard the voice of the fourth beast say, Come and see. 8 And I looked, and behold a pale horse: and his name that sat on him was **Death**, and Hell followed with him. And power was given unto them over the fourth part of the earth, to kill with sword, and with hunger, and with death, and with the beasts of the earth (emphasis added).

The fourth seal is a rider on a pale horse whose name is death. As this seal is opened ¼ of the earth is under the power of this rider to kill by wars, famines, and other catastrophes. It seems the ¼ quantity applies to the segment of the world under its control and not necessarily to the number who are actually killed. The next seal reveals people who have been martyred for their faith and could indicate that by now the Antichrist has demanded the world's worship.

> **Rev 6:9** And when he had opened the **fifth seal**, I saw under the altar the **souls of them that were slain for the word of God**, and for the testimony which they held: 10 And they cried with a loud voice, saying, **How long**, O Lord, holy and true, dost thou not judge and avenge our blood on them that dwell on the earth? 11 And white robes were given unto every one of them; and it was said unto them, that they should **rest yet for a little season**, until their fellow servants also and their brethren, that should be killed as they were, should be fulfilled (emphasis added).

As the fifth seal is opened the scene changes to heaven, and we are introduced to souls there who had been slain because of their faith. They are told to wait a little longer until the full numbers of martyrs are fulfilled.

> **Rev 6:12** And I beheld when he had opened the **sixth seal**, and, lo, there was a great earthquake; and the **sun** became black as sackcloth of hair, and the **moon** became as blood; 13 And the **stars** of heaven fell unto the earth, even as a fig tree casteth her untimely figs, when she is shaken of a mighty wind (emphasis added).

> **Rev 6:17** For the great **day of his wrath** is come; and who shall be able to stand? (emphasis added)

When the sixth seal is opened the sign of the Day of the Lord occurs - the sun turns dark, the moon turns red, and the stars fall from the sky, and God's wrath is proclaimed as having come.

> **Rev 8:1** And when he had opened the **seventh seal**, there was silence in heaven about the space of half an hour. 2 And I saw the seven angels which stood before God; and to them were given **seven trumpets**. 5 And the angel took the censer, and filled it with fire of the altar, and cast it into the earth... 6 And the seven angels which had the seven trumpets **prepared themselves to sound** (emphasis added).

As the seventh seal is broken, the angels with the seven trumpets prepare to sound them. The Day of the Lord's wrath has come. The seven trumpets begin to pour out God's wrath upon the world.

The Seals Compared to Matthew 24

We have made a quick overview of the seven seals of Revelation. A better understanding may be gained by comparing the seven seals to the events described in Matthew 24.

> **Matt 24:4** And Jesus answered and said unto them, Take heed that no man deceive you. 5 For many shall come in my name, saying, I am Christ; and shall deceive many.

The beginning of Matthew 24 could be connected to the rise of the Antichrist reviewed in the first seal.

Seal 1: Antichrist

Matthew 24 continues:

> **Matt 24:6** And ye shall hear of wars and rumours of wars: see that ye be not troubled: for all these things must come to pass, but the end is not yet. 7 For nation shall rise against nation, and kingdom against kingdom...

The second seal was the seal of war. The events of Matthew 24 begin to follow the sequence of the seals.

Seal 2: War

Matthew then predicts famine and pestilences. The third seal is the seal of famine.

Matt 24:7 ... and there shall be famines, and pestilences, and earthquakes, in divers places.

Seal 3: Famine

At this point, Matthew 24 makes a parenthetical statement: "All these are the beginning of birth pains." What follows is a description of persecution and death. Again, the seals match the sequence of Matthew 24.

> **Matt 24:8-10** (NIV) All these are the beginning of birth pains. {9} "Then you will be handed over to be persecuted and put to death, and you will be hated by all nations because of me. {10} At that time many will turn away from the faith and will betray and hate each other..."

Seal 4: Death

Matthew 24 then describes a period of suffering where these fourth and fifth seals will be opened. It says that this time of suffering will be unparalleled in all of history. As the fifth seal describes martyrs, Matthew 24 states that "you will be handed over to be persecuted and put to death" and the reason Jesus gives is "because of me."

> **Matt 24:21** For **then** shall be great tribulation, such as was not since the beginning of the world to this time, no, nor ever shall be. 22 And except those days should be shortened, there should no flesh be saved: but for the elect's sake those days shall be shortened (emphasis added).

Seal 5: Martyrs

In Matthew 24:10-20, describe a time of suffering, and by investigating these scriptures we can determine the timing of this terrible period of suffering and death.

> **(Mat 24:21-22 NIV) For then there will be great distress, unequaled from the beginning of the world until now--and never to be equaled again. {22} If those days had not been cut short, no one would survive, but for the sake of the elect those days will be shortened.**

Figure 19: At This Time

It is important to note the indicators Matthew uses to show the relation of time. In verse 9 he starts, "Then you will be handed over..." and then in verse 10 he states, "At that time many will turn away from the faith..." He continues in verse 21 "For then there will be great distress (NIV)..." All of these references center on verse 15:

> **Mat 24:15-16, 19** (NIV) **So** when you see standing in the holy place 'the **abomination that causes desolation**'... {16} then let those who are in Judea flee to the mountains... {19} How dreadful it will be in those days... (emphasis added)

145

Therefore, we can place the fourth and fifth seal suffering centered on the Abomination of Desolation. We know the Abomination of Desolation is the mid-point of the 70th Week when the Antichrist demands the world worship him. The suffering between the fourth and fifth seals, then, follows the Antichrist's demand for worship.

Matthew 24 vs. Revelation

(Matt 24:10-16 NIV) At that time many will turn away from the faith and will betray and hate each other... but he who stands firm to the end will be saved...

Figure 20: Suffering

Matt 24:5 (NIV) For many will come in my name, claiming, `I am the Christ,' and will deceive many. 6 You will hear of wars and rumors of wars, but see to it that you are not alarmed. Such things must happen, but the end is still to come. 7 Nation will rise against nation, and kingdom against kingdom. There will be famines and earthquakes in various places. 8 **All these are the beginning of birth pains**. 9 "Then you will be handed over to be persecuted and put to death, and you will be hated by all nations because of me. 10 At that time many will turn away from the faith and will betray and hate each other..." (emphasis added)

Matthew 24 defines the first through third seals as the "beginning of birth pains." So, we can illustrate the seals and the timing to look like figure 21.

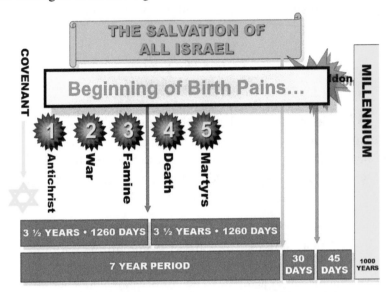

Figure 21: Birth Pains

Going back to Matthew 24, the next event in the passage is the sign of the Day of the Lord which corresponds to the sixth seal!

> **Matt 24:29** Immediately after the tribulation of those days shall the **sun be darkened, and the moon shall not give her light, and the stars shall fall from heaven,** and the powers of the heavens shall be shaken (emphasis added).

The six seal in the book of Revelation also depicts the sign of the Day of the Lord.

> **Rev 6:12** And I beheld when he had opened the sixth seal, and, lo, there was a great earthquake; and the **sun**

became black as sackcloth of hair, and the moon became as blood; 13 And the stars of heaven fell unto the earth, even as a fig tree casteth her untimely figs, when she is shaken of a mighty wind (emphasis added).

Seal 6: The Sign!

After the sign of the Day of the Lord which corresponds to the sixth seal of Revelation, Matthew 24 describes an event of gathering God's people. It describes the Son of Man coming on the clouds of the sky, a loud trumpet call and the gathering of His "elect" from all over the world.

> **Matt 24:30-31** (NIV) **At that time** the sign of the Son of Man will appear in the sky, and all the nations of the earth will mourn. They will see the Son of Man coming on the clouds of the sky, with power and great glory. {31} And he will send his angels with a loud trumpet call, and **they will gather his elect** from the four winds, from one end of the heavens to the other (emphasis added).

Matthew 24 then records the comparison of Noah's day and makes the statement "that is how it will be at the coming of the Son of Man."

> **Matt 24:37-38** (NIV) As it was in the days of Noah, so it will be at the coming of the Son of Man. {38} For in the days before the flood, people were eating and drinking, marrying and giving in marriage, up to the day Noah entered the ark; {39} and they knew nothing about what would happen until the flood came and took them all away. **That is how it will be at the coming of the**

Son of Man. {40} Two men will be in the field; one will be taken and the other left (emphasis added).

Following the sequence of events in Matthew 24 and detecting the connection of the fourth and fifth seals with the Abomination of Desolation helps us narrow down the rapture as happening after the sixth seal is opened which will happen after the Abomination of Desolation and the persecution of the Antichrist. This also means that the sixth seal and the sign of the Day of the Lord and the rapture will happen after the mid-point of the 70th Week of Daniel.

Following the 6th Seal: The Rapture

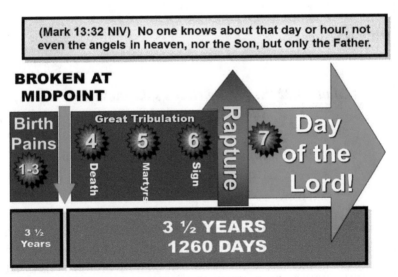

(Mark 13:32 NIV) No one knows about that day or hour, not even the angels in heaven, nor the Son, but only the Father.

BROKEN AT MIDPOINT

Birth Pains 1-3

Great Tribulation

4 Death

5 Martyrs

6 Sign

Rapture

7

Day of the Lord!

3 ½ Years

3 ½ YEARS 1260 DAYS

Figure 22: Rapture and Seals

Figure 22 depicts how the seven seals fall in the 70th Week of Daniel according to Matthew 24 and the book of Revelation. The exact timing of when each seal will happen is not clear except that the first three seals will happen before the mid-point, the fourth and fifth around or just after the mid-point, and the sixth and seventh seals after the mid-point.

Jesus told us in Mark 13:32 that no one knows the day and the hour. But He did say...

> **Matt 24:32** Now learn a parable of the fig tree; When his branch is yet tender, and putteth forth leaves, ye know that summer is nigh: 33 So likewise ye, **when ye shall see all these things, know that it is near, even at the doors.**

We can know His coming is "right at the door." So, we cannot say exactly when during the final half of the 70th Week the rapture will occur - but according to Matthew 24 it will be sometime during the second 3½ years. Jesus did give us two exciting clues as to when it would happen:

Two Clues...

Matt 24:22 "...for the elect's sake those days shall be shortened."

Matt 24:29 "Immediately after the tribulation of those days..."

We can say the tribulation of the second half of the 70th Week will be cut short for the elect (saints), and the rapture will take place immediately after the tribulation of those days. It helps us to realize why the New Testament writers would say, "even so, come quickly, Lord Jesus!"

There is one other important note when placing the timing of the rapture. It will happen before the 1st trumpet sounds and the seventh trumpet sounds at the end of the 70th Week. The fifth trumpet brings five months of torment to those on the earth. Therefore, presumably the rapture would have to happen at least six months prior to the end of the 70th Week for all the other trumpet judgments to fit.

In the last 3 1/2 years of the 70th week, the rapture could happen in as quickly as six months or less or as much as 2½ to 3 years. The fact that Jesus uses the word "immediately" causes this writer to believe the rapture will happen very early in the 2nd half of the 70th Week.

Chapter 10
The Wrath of God

In this chapter, we will deal with the events concerning the outpouring of God's wrath in the Day of the Lord. These events are foretold in the book of Revelation symbolized by the sounding of the seven trumpets and the pouring out of the seven bowls.

As we focus on the wrath of God, we will be focusing on the Day of the Lord after the saints of God are raptured from the earth to heaven.

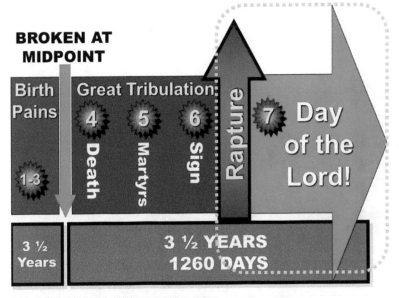

Figure 23: DOL Wrath

Rev 8:1 And when he had opened the **seventh seal**, there was silence in heaven about the space of half an hour. 2 And I saw the seven angels which stood before God; and to them were given **seven trumpets**. 3 And another angel came and stood at the altar, having a golden censer; and there was given unto him much incense, that he should offer [it] with the prayers of all saints upon the golden altar which was before the throne. 4 And the smoke of the incense, which came with the prayers of the saints, ascended up before God out of the angel's hand. 5 And the angel took the censer, and filled it with fire of the altar, and cast it into the earth: and there were voices, and thunderings, and lightnings, and an earthquake. 6 And **the seven angels which had the seven trumpets prepared themselves to sound** (emphasis added).

The division of the trumpets and bowls in the book of Revelation allow us to separate God's wrath into two parts we will call the "beginning wrath" and the "final wrath."

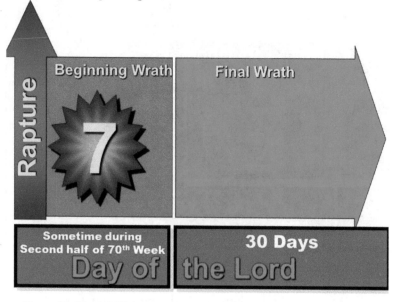

Figure 24: Wrath 2 Divisions

The wrath of God will begin as the seventh seal (Rev 8:1-6) on the scroll of "The Day of the Lord" is broken and the scroll is opened.

God's wrath begins with the sounding of the seven trumpets. When the sixth seal is opened we are told "the day of His wrath has come" (Rev. 6:17), and when the seventh seal is opened the seven trumpets begin to sound. The seven trumpets contain the beginning of God's wrath and most of them affect 1/3 of the earth.

The First Trumpet

Rev 8:7 The **first angel** sounded, and there followed hail and fire mingled with blood, and they were cast upon the earth: and the **third part of trees was burnt up, and all green grass was burnt up** (emphasis added).

As the first trumpet sounds a fiery hail storm burns up the earth. We are told 1/3 of the trees and all green grass are affected.

The Second Trumpet

Rev 8:8 And the **second angel** sounded, and as it were a great mountain burning with fire was cast into the sea: and the **third part of the sea** became blood; 9 And the third part of the creatures which were in the sea, and had life, died; and the third part of the ships were destroyed (emphasis added).

At the second trumpet sound, something like a volcano is described either erupting or crashing into the sea. It kills 1/3 of sea-life and turns 1/3 of the seas into blood. It is interesting to note part of this judgment includes 1/3 of all ships being destroyed. This is the only time during the trumpet judgments the targeted destruction of man-made items is mentioned.

The Third Trumpet

Rev 8:10 And the **third angel** sounded, and there fell a great star from heaven, burning as it were a lamp, and it fell upon the third part of the rivers, and upon the fountains of waters; 11 And the name of the star is called Wormwood: and the **third part of the waters** became wormwood; and many men died of the waters, because they were made bitter (emphasis added).

At the third trumpet sound, it appears a meteor or meteor shower strikes the earth and spoils 1/3 of all fresh water. Names in the Bible give meaning and significance - and here this meteor is named Wormwood. "Wormwood" is defined as "a nonpoisonous but bitter plant common to the Middle East. Wormwood often is used in analogy to speak of bitterness and sorrow."[1]

The Fourth Trumpet

Rev 8:12 And the **fourth angel** sounded, and **the third part of the sun** was smitten, and the **third part of the moon**, and the **third part of the stars**; so as the third part of them was darkened, and the day shone not for a third part of it, and the night likewise. 13 And I beheld,

156

and heard an angel flying through the midst of heaven, saying with a loud voice, **Woe, woe, woe**, to the inhabiters of the earth by reason of the other voices of the trumpet of the **three angels**, which are yet to sound! (emphasis added)

At the fourth trumpet sound, a third of the day and night become darkness. There is also a warning that things are about to get worse. The last three trumpets are introduced by three "woes." The designation of the judgments as "woes" indicates a greater degree of punishment to come than has so far happened.

The Fifth Trumpet

Rev 9:1 And the **fifth angel** sounded, and I saw a star fall from heaven unto the earth: and to him was given the key of the bottomless pit. 2 And he opened the bottomless pit; and there arose a smoke out of the pit, as the smoke of a great furnace; and the sun and the air were darkened by reason of the smoke of the pit. 3 And there came out of the smoke **locusts** upon the earth: and unto them was given power, as the scorpions of the earth have power. 4 And it was commanded them that they should not hurt the grass of the earth, neither any green thing, neither any tree; but only those men which have not the seal of God in their foreheads. 5 And to them it was given that they should not kill them, but **that they should be tormented five months**: and their torment was as the torment of a scorpion, when he striketh a man. 6 And in those days shall men seek death, and shall not find it; and shall desire to die, and death shall flee from them. 7 And the shapes of the locusts were like unto horses prepared unto battle; and on their heads

157

were as it were crowns like gold, and their faces were as the faces of men. 8 And they had hair as the hair of women, and their teeth were as the teeth of lions. 9 And they had breastplates, as it were breastplates of iron; and the sound of their wings was as the sound of chariots of many horses running to battle. 10 And they had tails like unto scorpions, and there were stings in their tails: and **their power was to hurt men five months.** 11 And they had a king over them, which is the angel of the bottomless pit, whose name in the Hebrew tongue is Abaddon, but in the Greek tongue hath his name Apollyon. 12 **One woe is past; and, behold, there come two woes more hereafter** (emphasis added).

The fifth trumpet is a judgment of "locusts." However, these locusts are not like any we have known. These locusts are released from the "bottomless pit" and are under orders to torment men that do not have the seal of God upon their foreheads. This is probably a reference to the 144,000 Jews that have been sealed, and it could include those who have accepted Christ after the rapture. It is interesting to note this fifth trumpet judgment has a span of time mentioned – five months. It is also emphasized by classifying it as a "woe," and a warning is cast regarding two more "woes" yet to come.

The Sixth Trumpet

Rev 9:13 And the **sixth angel** sounded, and I heard a voice from the four horns of the golden altar which is before God, 14 Saying to the sixth angel which had the trumpet, Loose the four angels which are bound in the great river Euphrates. 15 And the four angels were loosed, which were prepared for an hour, and a day, and a month, and a year, for to **slay the third part of men.**

16 And the number of the army of the horsemen were two hundred thousand thousand: and I heard the number of them. 17 And thus I saw the horses in the vision, and them that sat on them, having breastplates of fire, and of jacinth, and brimstone: and the heads of the horses were as the heads of lions; and out of their mouths issued fire and smoke and brimstone. 18 By these three was the **third part of men killed**, by the fire, and by the smoke, and by the brimstone, which issued out of their mouths. 19 For their power is in their mouth, and in their tails: for their tails were like unto serpents, and had heads, and with them they do hurt. 20 And the rest of the men which were not killed by these plagues yet **repented not** of the works of their hands, that they should not worship devils, and idols of gold, and silver, and brass, and stone, and of wood: which neither can see, nor hear, nor walk: 21 **Neither repented** they of their murders, nor of their sorceries, nor of their fornication, nor of their thefts.

At the sixth trumpet 200,000,000 mounted, supernatural troops are sent throughout the world. The description declares this judgment to have been prepared for specifically this hour, day, month and year. These fire-breathing horses are said to have the heads of lions and tails like snakes. The result is 1/3 of mankind suffer terrible, painful deaths. The sixth trumpet is the second woe and one more is yet to come.

The narrative of the sixth trumpet concludes with the indictment of the wickedness of mankind in spite of the devastation of the judgments of God. The scripture teaches the rapture as being an obvious event which is seen by the entire world. There will be no question that these judgments are sent by God. They will have seen Jesus on the clouds, the rapture of God's people, and they will have gone through six trumpet judgments; nevertheless, they still do not repent.

The point given in verses 20 and 21 regarding man's refusal to repent provide another glimpse into God's purpose for these devastating judgments. His desire is for mankind to repent. It recalls Joel 2:12 where the Lord describes the Day of the Lord and says, "Even now... return to me with all your heart" (NIV).

The Small Scroll

> **Rev 10:1-3** (NIV) Then I saw another mighty angel coming down from heaven. He was robed in a cloud, with a rainbow above his head; his face was like the sun, and his legs were like fiery pillars. {2} He was holding a **little scroll**, which lay open in his hand. He planted his right foot on the sea and his left foot on the land, {3} and he gave a loud shout like the roar of a lion. When he shouted, the voices of the seven thunders spoke. (emphasis added)

After the sixth trumpet sounds and in preparation for the seventh trumpet, we are introduced to a small scroll.

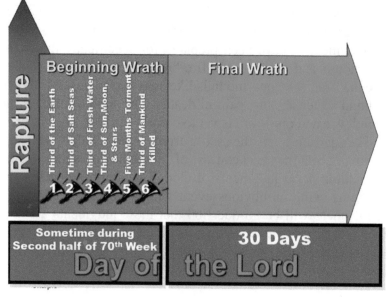

Figure 25: 6 Trumpets

The appearance of this scroll provides a transition revealing the events of the large scroll are drawing to a close, and a final set of events are about to take place. The small scroll signifies God's beginning wrath is finished and His final wrath is about to commence.

The small scroll signifies the work of the large scroll is complete and now the small scroll is opened. Following is a list of the events completed by the large scroll and relates to the list to be accomplished during the 70th Week given in Daniel 9:24.

Figure 26: Small Scroll

Events Completed by Large Scroll

- Daniel's 70th Week is completed (Dan 9:24)
- Israel's transgression will be completed
- Israel's sin will be ended
- Israel's iniquity will be atoned for
- The Times of the Gentiles will be fulfilled (Luke 21:24)
- The Fullness of the Gentiles will have come in (Rom 11:25)

- The first woe is completed (Rev. 9:12)
- The 6th Trumpet Judgment is finished (Rev. 11:13-19)
- The 3½ year ministry of the two witnesses will be done (Rev 11:7)

The small scroll signifies the sounding of the seventh trumpet which is the completion of the beginning wrath of God. As the seventh trumpet is about to sound, an angel declares there will be no more delay.

> **Revelation 10:4** (NIV) And when the seven thunders spoke, I was about to write; but I heard a voice from heaven say, "Seal up what the seven thunders have said and do not write it down." {5} Then the angel I had seen standing on the sea and on the land raised his right hand to heaven. {6} And he swore by him who lives for ever and ever, who created the heavens and all that is in them, the earth and all that is in it, and the sea and all that is in it, and said, "**There will be no more delay!** {7} But in the days when the **seventh angel is about to sound his trumpet**, the mystery of God will be accomplished, just as he announced to his servants the prophets." {8} Then the voice that I had heard from heaven spoke to me once more: "Go, take the scroll that lies open in the hand of the angel who is standing on the sea and on the land." {9} So I went to the angel and asked him to give me the little scroll. He said to me, "Take it and eat it. **It will turn your stomach sour**, but in your mouth it will **be as sweet as honey."** {10} I took the little scroll from the angel's hand and ate it. It tasted **as sweet as honey** in my mouth, but when I had eaten it, **my stomach turned sour** (emphasis added).

The Apostle John is told to take the small scroll and eat it. As he is told, it tastes as sweet as honey; however, it turns sour in his stomach. This may be how we describe an event as being "bittersweet." The scroll contains events that are both sweet and sour/bitter.

Sweet

- God's gracious redemption of Israel
- The completion of the spiritual Kingdom of God

Sour

- Final wrath of God
- Worst ever to be poured out on man

Contained in the small scroll is the final redemption of Israel and the completion of God kingdom, but also the final wrath of God upon the world which has rejected Him.

Rev 10:11 - 11:7 (NIV) Then I was told, "You must **prophesy again** about many peoples, nations, languages and kings." {11:1} I was given a reed like a measuring rod and was told, "Go and measure the temple of God and the altar, and count the worshipers there. {2} But exclude the outer court; do not measure it, because it has been given to the **Gentiles. They will trample on the holy city for 42 months.** {3} And I will give power to my two witnesses, and they will prophesy for **1,260 days,** clothed in sackcloth... {5} If anyone tries to harm them, fire comes from their mouths and devours their enemies. This is how anyone who wants to harm them must die. {6} These men have power to shut up the sky so that it will not rain during the time they are prophesying; and they have power to turn the waters into blood and to strike the earth with every kind of plague as often as they want. {7} **Now when they have finished**

163

their testimony, the beast that comes up from the Abyss will attack them, and overpower and kill them" (emphasis added).

The ministry of the two witnesses which began 1,260 days ago is about to be finished. As the large scroll completes, the two witnesses are killed and the 30 day reclamation period begins.

> **Rev 11:11** And after three days and an half the Spirit of life from God entered into them, and they stood upon their feet; and great fear fell upon them which saw them. 12 And they heard a great voice from heaven saying unto them, Come up hither. And they ascended up to heaven in a cloud; and their enemies beheld them. 13 And the same hour was there a great earthquake, and the tenth part of the city fell, and in the earthquake were slain of men seven thousand: and the remnant were affrighted, and gave glory to the God of heaven. 14 **The second woe is past; and, behold, the third woe cometh quickly** (emphasis added).

The appearance of the small scroll signifies the completion of the events of Daniel's 70th Week contained in the large scroll, it also signifies the beginning of the 30 day period following the 70th Week and the events to follow (figure 27).

Events Initiated by the Small Scroll

- The 30 day Reclamation period begins (Dan 12:11)
- Everlasting righteousness will be brought in to Israel (Dan 9:24)
- Seal up vision and prophecy (Dan 9:24)
- Death and resurrection of two witnesses (Rev 11:7,11-12)
- The second woe is completed (Rev 11:14)

164

- The seventh trumpet is sounded: the third woe begins (Rev 11:15)
- Almighty God begins His reign over earth (Rev 11:17)
- The last of God's wrath begins (Rev 11:18, 15:1)

As the small scroll begins, the seventh trumpet is about to sound. This is the last "woe" and will contain the final judgment of God in the form of the seven bowls.

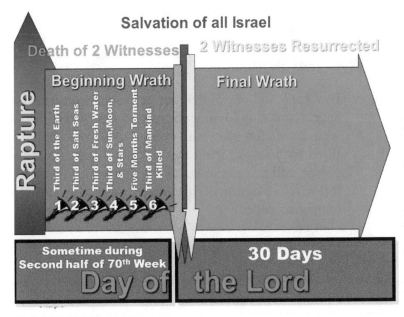

Figure 27: Initiates Small Scroll

The Seventh Trumpet

Rev 11:15 And the **seventh angel** sounded; and there were great voices in heaven, saying, The kingdoms of this world are become the kingdoms of our Lord, and of his Christ; and he shall reign for ever and ever (emphasis added).

Furthermore, the seventh trumpet indicates Christ is re-claiming His rule over the earth. The end of the 70th Week signifies the salvation of all Israel and the preparation for Christ to rule the earth.

> **Rev 15:1** (NIV) I saw in heaven another great and marvelous sign: seven angels with the **seven last plagues**--last, **because with them God's wrath is completed**. (emphasis added)

The Final Wrath

> **Rev 15:7** And one of the four beasts gave unto the seven angels **seven golden vials full of the wrath of God**, who liveth for ever and ever. 8 And the temple was filled with smoke from the glory of God, and from his power; and no man was able to enter into the temple, till the seven plagues of the seven angels were fulfilled (emphasis added).

Now, the final wrath of God will be poured out upon those dwelling on the earth. It is symbolized by seven golden bowls or vials that will be poured out upon mankind. It has been stated these judgments will happen quickly, possibly in as little as 25 days.

The First Bowl

> **Rev 16:1-2** (NIV) Then I heard a loud voice from the temple saying to the seven angels, "Go, pour out the seven bowls of God's wrath on the earth." {2} The **first**

angel went and poured out his bowl on the land, and **ugly and painful sores broke out** on the people who had the mark of the beast and worshiped his image. (emphasis added)

As the bowl judgments begin, it is interesting to note this is the first mention of the mark of the beast as it applies to God's wrath beginning to pour out. It leads this writer to conclude the mark of the beast may not be implemented until after the rapture. Also notice the "sores" of this judgment, because they will be mentioned again.

The Second Bowl

Rev 16:3 And the **second angel** poured out his vial upon the **sea; and it became as the blood of a dead man: and every living soul died in the sea** (emphasis added).

Whereas the trumpets affected 1/3 of the seas, waters, earth, etc. The bowls now affect everything. Imagine the impact of "every living thing in the sea" dying. This would have a global impact. The magnitude of every living creature in the sea dying would be catastrophic.

The Third Bowl

Rev 16:4 And the **third angel** poured out his vial upon the **rivers and fountains of waters; and they became blood.** 5 And I heard the angel of the waters say, Thou art righteous, O Lord, which art, and wast, and shalt be, because thou hast judged thus. 6 **For they have shed the blood of saints and prophets**, and thou hast given them blood to drink; for they are worthy. 7 And I heard another out of the altar say, Even so, Lord God Almighty, true and righteous are thy judgments (emphasis added).

Now, not only is the salt sea impacted, but all fresh water. Again, the tremendous pace at which these judgments happen must be emphasized. How long can mankind survive without a source of fresh water?

The Fourth Bowl

Rev 16:8 And the **fourth angel** poured out his vial upon the **sun; and power was given unto him to scorch men with fire**. 9 And men were scorched with great heat, and blasphemed the name of God, which hath power over these plagues: and they repented not to give him glory (emphasis added).

The fourth bowl is a judgment of intense heat. Even in the agony of judgment people blaspheme God, and they are still are hard-hearted and refuse to repent. In the pouring out of His wrath, God's goal is for people to finally recognize Him and repent of their selfish ways.

The Fifth Bowl

Rev 16:10 And the **fifth angel** poured out his vial upon the seat of the beast; and **his kingdom was full of darkness**; and they gnawed their tongues for pain, 11

And blasphemed the God of heaven **because of their pains and their sores**, and repented not of their deeds (emphasis added).

The fifth bowl is a judgment of darkness, and it is especially targeted at the "seat" or the throne (NIV and NAS) of the Antichrist. The description of the "pain and sores" refers back to the first bowl judgment, which shows the rapid progression of these judgments. The darkness of this judgment is ironic as the scripture declares men loved darkness rather than light (John 3:19).

The Sixth Bowl

Rev 16:12 And the **sixth angel** poured out his vial upon the great river Euphrates; and the water thereof was dried up, **that the way of the kings of the east might be prepared**. 13 And I saw three unclean spirits like frogs come out of the mouth of the dragon, and out of the mouth of the beast, and out of the mouth of the false prophet. 14 For they are the spirits of devils, working miracles, **which go forth unto the kings of the earth and of the whole world, to gather them to the battle of that great day of God Almighty**. 15 Behold, I come as a thief. Blessed is he that watcheth, and keepeth his garments, lest he walk naked, and they see his shame. 16 **And he gathered them together into a place called in the Hebrew tongue Armageddon** (emphasis added).

The sixth bowl prepares the earth for the great battle of Armageddon. The image of the frogs implies that there will be a demonic influence drawing all the kings of the earth to the place of Armageddon. The Antichrist – beast and false prophet meet their "end" at Armageddon and then the seventh bowl completes the wrath of God.

The Seventh Bowl

Rev 16:17-21 (NIV) The **seventh angel** poured out his bowl into the air, and out of the temple came a loud voice from the throne, saying, **"It is done!"** {18} **Then there came flashes of lightning, rumblings, peals of thunder and a severe earthquake.** No earthquake like it has ever occurred since man has been on earth, **so tremendous was the quake.** {19} The great city split into three parts, and the **cities of the nations collapsed.** God remembered Babylon the Great and gave her the cup filled with the wine of the fury of his wrath. {20} Every island fled away and the **mountains could not be found.** {21} From the sky **huge hailstones of about a hundred pounds each fell upon men.** And they cursed God on account of the plague of hail, because the plague was so terrible. (emphasis added)

The seventh bowl contains a global earthquake and huge hailstones that fall on men. The seventh bowl is said to level mountains and remove islands from their place. This last bowl judgment indicates global devastation. Again, rather than repent in the face of judgment, the response is to curse God.

God's final bowl of wrath is dispensed, and as the wrath of God is completed; we need to note some specifics about the bowl judgments.

The Bowl Judgments

- They happen quickly possibly in as little as 25 days
- The trumpet judgments affect 1/3 of mankind
- The bowl judgments affect all mankind

Armageddon

The Battle of Armageddon is one of the major events surrounding the return of Christ discussed at the end of chapter one. This battle is the final showdown for the Antichrist and the False Prophet. God's judgment is complete and following the Battle of Armageddon, the 45 day restoration period begins.

Rev 19:17 And I saw an angel standing in the sun; and he cried with a loud voice, saying to all the fowls that fly in the midst of heaven, Come and gather yourselves together unto the supper of the great God; 18 That ye may eat the flesh of kings, and the flesh of captains, and the flesh of mighty men, and the flesh of horses, and of them that sit on them, and the flesh of all men, both free and bond, both small and great. 19 **And I saw the beast, and the kings of the earth, and their armies, gathered together to make war against him that sat on the horse, and against his army.** 20 And **the beast was taken, and with him the false prophet** that wrought miracles before him, with which he deceived them that had received the mark of the beast, and them that worshipped his image. **These both were cast alive into a lake of fire burning with brimstone.** 21 And the remnant were slain with the sword of him that sat upon the horse, which [sword] proceeded out of his mouth: and all the fowls were filled with their flesh (emphasis added).

Figure 28 displays the complete picture of the wrath that is poured out when the Day of the Lord commences.

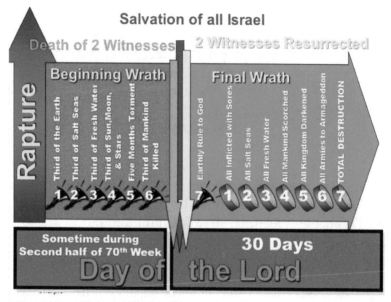

Figure 28: DOL Wrath

---

[1] Trent C. Butler, *Holman Bible Dictionary* (Nashville, TN: Holman Bible Publishers, 1991), 1421.

Chapter 11
The Pre-Wrath Perspective

In concluding the pre-wrath teaching, there are some significant points regarding the pre-wrath rapture and prophecy to emphasize. These points will help clarify the pre-wrath position, solidify scriptural support, and differentiate the pre-wrath position from other views.

Scriptural Basis for Timing

The Bible is clear no one can know the "day" or the "hour" when the Lord Jesus will return. However, the scripture does say we may know the time is at hand and even "at the door." The Pre-wrath view sees the rapture happening sometime during the early to middle part of second half of Daniel's 70th Week. Some scriptures which support a Pre-wrath timing are listed below.

- *The sign of the Day of the Lord reveals the timing – especially Matthew 24 & Revelation 6*

- *2 Thessalonians 2 – it will come after Antichrist is revealed*

- *Jesus said to watch for the Abomination of Desolation – Matthew 24:15*

Wrath or Tribulation?

We said in a post-tribulation view God's people endure the wrath of God, yet the scriptures clearly tell us God's people will be delivered from God's wrath. This would seem to be a problem for the pre-wrath view also. Is the second half of the 70th Week, also called the "great tribulation" God's wrath?

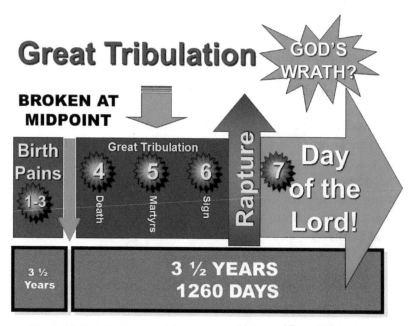

Figure 29: Tribulation or Wrath?

We reviewed the scriptures about God's people being rescued from God's wrath:

> **Romans 5:9** Much more then, being now justified by his blood, we shall be saved from wrath through him.

> **1 Thess 1:10** (NIV) and to wait for his Son from heaven, whom he raised from the dead--Jesus, who rescues us from the coming wrath.

1 Thess 5:9 For God hath not appointed us to wrath, but to obtain salvation by our Lord Jesus Christ

Rev 3:10 (NIV) Since you have kept my command to endure patiently, I will also keep you from the hour of trial that is going to come upon the whole world to test those who live on the earth.

We know the Day of the Lord is an outpouring of God's wrath, but is God's wrath poured out before the Day of the Lord begins? We know Christians will be persecuted; are they not suffering the wrath of God? Although the seals contain wars and death, the book of Revelation does not mention the wrath of God until the sixth seal is broken. Do the prior seals contain the wrath of God? The Bible tells us in Revelation chapter 12...

Rev 12:7 And there was war in heaven: Michael and his angels fought against the dragon; and the dragon fought and his angels, 8 And prevailed not; **neither was their place found any more in heaven**. 9 And the great dragon was cast out, that old serpent, called the Devil, and Satan, which deceiveth the whole world: he was **cast out into the earth**, and his angels were cast out with him (emphasis added).

Rev 12:12 Therefore rejoice, ye heavens, and ye that dwell in them. Woe to the inhabiters of the earth and of the sea! for the devil is come down unto you, having **great wrath**, because he knoweth that he hath but a short time (emphasis added).

Revelation 12 flashes back to the war in heaven between Satan and the angels. The scripture declares the devil has come down to earth having great wrath. God's wrath is not mentioned in the book of Revelation before the sixth seal and the Day of the Lord. But, the seals do tell us the tragic events that will take place on earth under the reign of Antichrist. Therefore, it is evident God's wrath is poured out after the Day of the Lord begins, but it is the wrath of Satan which takes place before the Day of the Lord.

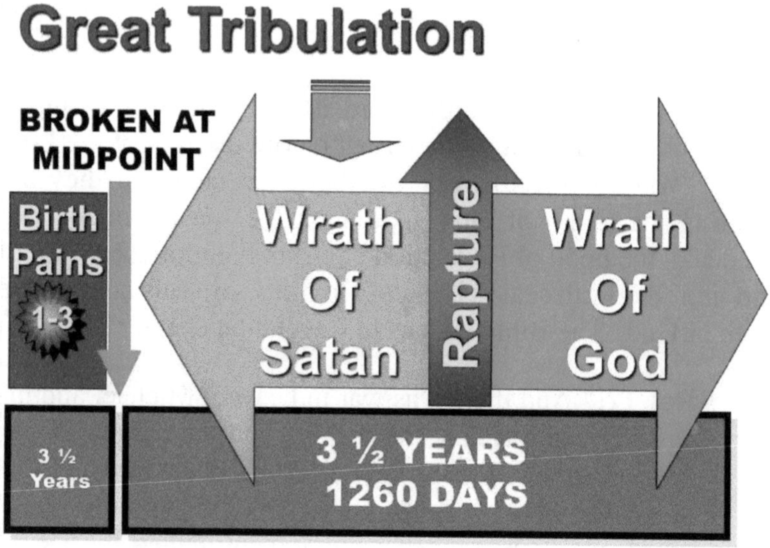

Figure 30: Wrath of Satan

There are two concepts of affliction that are portrayed in the end-time prophecies. The Bible teaches in Matthew 24 there will be great tribulation. The book of Revelation has much to say about the outpouring of the wrath of God. One must separate these two concepts by determining the target of the affliction. The tribulation of Matthew 24 is focused against the people of God; however, the wrath of the book of Revelation is against the wicked of the world who have rejected God. Therefore, it becomes clear that there is a distinction between the wrath of God and the wrath of Satan against God. There is one other passage which seems to interfere with this idea.

> **Luke 21:36** (NIV) Be always on the watch, and pray that you may be able to **escape all that is about to**

happen, and that you may be able to stand before the Son of Man. (emphasis added)

This verse tells us we may escape ALL that is about to happen. Does this mean persecution too? Let us go back to the scripture.

> **Luke 21:25** And there shall be signs in the sun, and in the moon, and in the stars; ... 27 And then shall they see the Son of man coming in a cloud with power and great glory. 28 And when these things begin to come to pass, then look up, and lift up your heads; for your redemption draweth nigh.

> **Luke 21:34-36** (NIV) Be careful, or your hearts will be weighed down with dissipation, drunkenness and the anxieties of life, and **that day** will close on you unexpectedly like a trap. {35} **For it will come upon all those who live on the face of the whole earth**. {36} Be always on the watch, and pray that you may be able to **escape all that is about to happen, [referring to "that day"]** and that you may be able to stand before the Son of Man. (emphasis added)

Now we see in verse 34 we are talking about "that day" and that day IS the Day of the Lord. Those who love Jesus WILL escape all that is about to happen on "that day" - we will have already been raptured!

Unmistakable Return of Christ

Upon examining the pre-tribulation view the rapture was thought to be a secret disappearance of Christians throughout the world. The secret disappearance idea conflicts with Jesus' teaching not to listen if someone claims Jesus had already come because His coming would be like the lightning flashing from East to West.

According to the pre-wrath view, when Jesus raptures the church it will not be a secret appearance. When He comes in the clouds it WILL be like the lightning flashing from east to west. People WILL disappear as they are "caught up" to be with the Lord; however, everyone will know what is happening. This was revealed in the book of Revelation:

> **Rev 6:14** And the heaven departed as a scroll when it is rolled together; and every mountain and island were moved out of their places. 15 And the kings of the earth, and the great men, and the rich men, and the chief captains, and the mighty men, and every bondman, and every free man, hid themselves in the dens and in the rocks of the mountains; 16 And said to the mountains and rocks, **Fall on us, and hide us from the face of him that sitteth on the throne, and from the wrath of the Lamb**: 17 For the great day of his wrath is come; and who shall be able to stand? (emphasis added)

The time for God to do things anonymously is past when the Day of the Lord comes. There will be no question anymore if there is a God, or Who He is. The rebellion of the world will be a final obvious rebellion against God Himself.

The Question of the Restrainer

The pre-tribulation view teaches the restrainer IS the Holy Spirit, and He will be removed with the church at the rapture.

> **2 Thess 2:6-8** (NIV) And now you know what is holding him back, **so that he may be revealed at the proper time**. {7} For the secret power of lawlessness is already at work; but **the one who now holds it back will continue to do so till he is taken out of the way.**

{8} **And then** the lawless one will be revealed, whom the Lord Jesus will overthrow with the breath of his mouth and destroy by the splendor of his coming. (emphasis added)

This assumption was reviewed in chapter five. The pre-tribulation view asserts at the Rapture, the Holy Spirit is removed from the world with the church allowing the Antichrist the freedom to reveal himself to the world. This assumption is not supported by scripture. The question remains, "Who is this Restrainer?" The Bible gives us a clue as to another possibility. The prophet Daniel writes about the archangel Michael:

> **Dan 12:1** (NIV) **"At that time Michael**, the great prince **who protects your people, will arise. There will be a time of distress** such as has not happened from the beginning of nations until then. **But at that time** your people--everyone whose name is found written in the book--**will be delivered"** (emphasis added).

In Daniel there is a verse identifying this particular episode of the end of time as "a time of distress such as has not happened from the beginning of the nations until then." This same phrase is also in Matthew 24.

> **Matt 24:21** For then shall be great tribulation, such as was not since the beginning of the world to this time, no, nor ever shall be.

Michael the archangel is identified as the one who protects "your people." He will "arise." That word can be translated "to stand" or "to stop."[1] Whatever else it means, when Michael "stands" it initiates this time of distress. The strongest scriptural evidence is Michael, rather than the Holy Spirit, is the restrainer.

179

Immanency

Particularly adamant in the pre-tribulation view is the doctrine of immanency. Those who hold to a pre-tribulation rapture promote the teaching that the coming of Christ is an imminent event. Immanency is defined as follows:

> "An imminent event is one that is always hanging overhead, is constantly ready to befall or overtake a person, is always close at hand in the sense that it could happen at any moment. Other things may happen before the imminent event, but nothing else must take place before it happens. If something else must take place before an event can happen, that event is not imminent. The necessity of something else taking place first destroys the concept of immanency."[2]

Key elements to immanency...

- *The certainty that the Lord may come at any moment*

- *The uncertainty of the timing of His arrival*

- *The fact that no prophesied event stands between the believer and that hour*[3]

Immanency is based upon scriptures such as these:

James 5:7-9 (NIV) Be patient, then, brothers, until the Lord's coming. See how the farmer waits for the land to yield its valuable crop and how patient he is for the autumn and spring rains. {8} You too, be patient and stand firm, because **the Lord's coming is near**. {9} Don't grumble against each other, brothers, or you will be judged. **The Judge is standing at the door**! (emphasis added)

Phil 4:5 Let your moderation be known unto all men. **The Lord is at hand** (emphasis added).

1 Cor 1:7 (NIV) Therefore you do not lack any spiritual gift as you **eagerly wait** for our Lord Jesus Christ to be revealed. (emphasis added)

The main argument for immanency is how the scripture records the Lord's return as being "near." He could come at any moment. The scriptures also state God's people eagerly waited for the Lord's return. However, there is a passage in Zephaniah stating the Day of the Lord is also near.

Zephaniah 1:14 (NIV) The great day of the LORD is near-- near and coming quickly. Listen! ...

This passage was written 400 years before Jesus was born. Using the same reasoning a conclusion could be made the Day of the Lord is also imminent! But scriptures tell us there are several things that must happen before the Day of the Lord.

Joel 2:31 The sun shall be turned into darkness, and the moon into blood, **before** the great and the terrible day of the LORD come (emphasis added).

Malachi 4:5 Behold, I will send you Elijah the prophet **before** the coming of the great and dreadful day of the LORD (emphasis added).

2 Thess 2:3 (NIV) Don't let anyone deceive you in any way, for that day will not come **until** the rebellion occurs and the man of lawlessness is revealed, the man doomed to destruction (emphasis added).

The definition of immanency quoted earlier and the scriptures listed above make the return of Christ unable to be an imminent event.

"...If something else must take place before an event can happen, that event is not imminent. The necessity of something else taking place first destroys the concept of immanency."[4]

Jesus coming is near in the same way the prophets proclaimed the Day of the Lord is near. There are prophecies which have to take place before the Day of the Lord, and so the Day of the Lord is NOT imminent.

Is there anything that has to happen before Jesus comes – "yes!" If His coming is the Day of the Lord then there is a sign in the sun, moon, and stars, and the appearing of Antichrist and the coming of Elijah must come first - so His coming is not imminent. However, how do we answer the question, "Could Jesus come now?"

I also believe the answer is "yes." Even though there are events that must come first; I believe these events could fall into place very quickly - maybe even without notice.

The Day of the Lord – A Known Doctrine

Another aspect of the pre-wrath teaching is the importance of the doctrine of the Day of the Lord. Although there is scant teaching on the Day of the Lord today, the scriptures indicate it was a well-known and accepted teaching in the Old Testament and the New Testament.

The Old Testament prophet Amos records the following verse implying the Day of the Lord was a common teaching and anticipated by the religious public.

> **Amos 5:18** Woe unto you that desire the day of the LORD! to what end is it for you? the day of the LORD is darkness, and not light. 19 As if a man did flee from a lion, and a bear met him; or went into the house, and leaned his hand on the wall, and a serpent bit him.

Furthermore, the Apostle Paul alluded to the familiarity of the church with the teaching of the Day of the Lord in his letter to the Thessalonians.

> **1 Thess 5:1** (NIV) Now, brothers, about times and dates we do not need to write to you, 2 for **you know very well** that the day of the Lord will come like a thief in the night (emphasis added).

Not only does he state they were familiar with the Day of the Lord, but he indicates they knew the teaching "very well." It becomes even more obvious the Day of the Lord was an important teaching when one considers all the verses having more vague allusions like "that day," or the "day of wrath." Some examples are:

> **Job 20:27** The heaven shall reveal his iniquity; and the earth shall rise up against him. 28 The increase of his house shall depart, and his goods shall flow away in the day of his wrath. 29 This is the portion of a wicked man from God, and the heritage appointed unto him by God.

> **Psalm 110:5** The Lord at thy right hand shall strike through kings in the day of his wrath. 6 He shall judge among the heathen, he shall fill the places with the dead bodies; he shall wound the heads over many countries.

Prov 11:4 Riches profit not in the day of wrath: but righteousness delivereth from death.

Isaiah 13:13 Therefore I will shake the heavens, and the earth shall remove out of her place, in the wrath of the LORD of hosts, and in the day of his fierce anger.

Ezekiel 7:19 They shall cast their silver in the streets, and their gold shall be removed: their silver and their gold shall not be able to deliver them in the day of the wrath of the LORD: they shall not satisfy their souls, neither fill their bowels: because it is the stumblingblock of their iniquity.

Zephaniah 2:1 Gather yourselves together, yea, gather together, O nation not desired; 2 Before the decree bring forth, before the day pass as the chaff, before the fierce anger of the LORD come upon you, before the day of the LORD'S anger come upon you.

Rom 2:5 But after thy hardness and impenitent heart treasurest up unto thyself wrath against the day of wrath and revelation of the righteous judgment of God;

The Day of the Lord is solidified even stronger when the passage in the book of Revelation is added which refers to the day of the wrath of the Lamb finally having come.

Rev 6:16 And said to the mountains and rocks, Fall on us, and hide us from the face of him that sitteth on the throne, and from the wrath of the Lamb: 17 For the great day of his wrath is come; and who shall be able to stand?

The Mark of the Beast

The Mark of the Beast is probably one of the most well-known elements of the second coming of Christ. There are some aspects of this mark worth noting. One must understand this mark is more than simply an identification mark. The mark seals the eternal destiny of the one who receives the mark. The scripture makes this clear.

> **Revelation 14:9** And the third angel followed them, saying with a loud voice, If any man worship the beast and his image, and receive his mark in his forehead, or in his hand, 10 The same shall drink of the wine of the wrath of God, which is poured out without mixture into the cup of his indignation; and he shall be tormented with fire and brimstone in the presence of the holy angels, and in the presence of the Lamb: 11 And the smoke of their torment ascendeth up for ever and ever: and they have no rest day nor night, who worship the beast and his image, and whosoever receiveth the mark of his name.

Therefore, to receive the mark of the beast is to reject God. Secondly, the mark serves as a sign for judgment as God's final wrath is poured out upon the earth. We are told the first two bowl judgments are directly aimed at those who have received the mark of the beast.

Now, as we contemplate the mark of the beast, there are a couple of questions for which there are no explicit answers. First, can a Christian be forced to take the mark and would doing so cause him to lose his salvation? Second, when during the unfolding of events, will the mark of the beast take place?

In answer to the first question, the scripture would seem to indicate the mark is forced upon people according to the NIV version of Revelation 13:16.

> **Revelation 13:16** (NIV) He also forced everyone, small and great, rich and poor, free and slave, to receive a mark on his right hand or on his forehead, 17 so that no one could buy or sell unless he had the mark, which is the name of the beast or the number of his name.

But the word "forced" is the word "poieō" which means "to make, do, cause, effect, bring about..."[5] Even though the word means "to make" it is more along the meaning of "to bring about" rather than "to force." The word translated "to receive" is the word "didōmi" which means "to give."[6] Therefore a more accurate rendering might be like the KJV "he caused... to give them a mark." Also, in Rev 14:9 it says "...If anyone worships the beast and his image and receives his mark on the forehead or on the hand..." there seems to be the sense the mark has to be taken willingly. Furthermore, in the first bowl judgment it says "painful sores broke out on the people who had the mark and worshipped his image." There is a sense where these two activities of worshipping the beast and receiving the mark go together.

> **Revelation 14:9** And the third angel followed them, saying with a loud voice, If any man worship the beast and his image, **and** receive his mark in his forehead, or in his hand, 10 The same shall drink of the wine of the wrath of God, which is poured out without mixture into the cup of his indignation (emphasis added).

Again, the receiving of the mark is linked to worshipping the beast. It may be the mark itself, even if it were forced, would not be enough to condemn a soul. The scripture does say in Rev 14:11 (NIV) "...There is no rest day or night for those who worship the beast and his image, or for anyone who receives the mark of his name." The "or" would lead one to believe the mark would be enough, but the word "or" here is "kai" normally translated "and."

So, it may very well be the mark alone would not be enough and may explain why the mark could not be forced. Now, the question remains, when will the mark of the beast take place in the unfolding of events?

The Mark of the Beast is not mentioned in any of the judgments until the final wrath in the form of the bowl judgments. These will not take place until the end of the 70th Week of Daniel. Furthermore, in the fifth trumpet judgment which consists of the locust creatures, the creatures are told not to harm the grass or any plants, but only those people who did not have the seal of God on their foreheads (Rev. 9:4). This leads the writer to believe the Mark of the Beast would not have been instituted by this point, or it would have been the indicator of punishment as it is in the bowl judgments. No one can be dogmatic on this point, but the writer believes the weight of scripture leads to this conclusion.

The Urgency of the Pre-wrath Message

Why is the pre-wrath view important? Does it really matter if a person believes pre-wrath or pre-tribulation? There is a very significant reason why the pre-wrath view is not only important but urgent. The scriptures spend a lot of time providing information about the Day of the Lord and Jesus' return. Jesus, Himself, warned numerous times to watch and be ready, and also to be careful you are not deceived.

The urgency of the pre-wrath view is much of the church today has bought in totally believing the Bible teaches that Christians will not be present when the Antichrist appears on the scene. Popular accepted teaching is Christians will be raptured before the Antichrist appears. Therefore, if the correct biblical teaching is, in fact, the Antichrist WILL come first – the modern church is being set up for deception. Can you imagine a world ruler who seemingly has all the answers for society's ills – the most charismatic figure ever to appear? Can you imagine by the time he demands the world worship him, how much of the church will already be emotionally vested in him.

Whether you agree with the pre-wrath view or not, we should all be ready to be alert, watch and not be deceived even if things do not turn out the way we expect.

---

[1] Samuel Prideaux Tregelles, *Gesenius Hebrew and Chaldee Lexicon to the Old Testament Scriptures* (Grand Rapids, MI: Baker Book House, 1979), 637.

[2] Renald Showers, *Maranatha*, (New Jersey: Friends of Israel Gospel Ministry, Inc., 1995) 127.

[3] Charles Cooper, *Imminency: A Phantom Doctrine!*, The Sign Ministries, Inc., 2000) 1.

[4] Showers, 127.

[5] Barclay M. Newman, *A Concise Greek-English Dictionary of the New Testament* (London: United Bible Societies, 1971), 145-146.

[6] Ibid., 45.

Epilogue

As I have studied and read on the Pre-wrath rapture and the Day of the Lord, I found for the first time all prophecies seem to naturally fit together. There actually does seem to be a plan for Jesus' Second Coming which makes sense throughout the Bible. I found myself no longer having to settle for an explanation how things will just "pan-out." I found I could intellectually defend what the Bible teaches.

Do I have all the answers? Certainly not! In fact, I am sure some of what I have concluded may be wrong. But, the sense and harmony I find in scriptural prophecy from the prewrath perspective, and the conclusive amount of scriptural support assure I am closer to scriptural truth than I have ever been before.

One day I was talking to a college student, and he was asking me about the return of Christ. I began to share with him through Matthew 24 the sense of the pre-wrath teaching. As I finished his eyes got wide and he exclaimed, "This makes all the sense in the world! Why are you not shouting this from the mountaintops?" I answered, people do not want to know the truth. They are happier to think God will save them from any persecution or difficulty. I admitted, I would love to be wrong, because I would rather miss it too. But this is just not what I see the scripture teaching. I am reminded of what the Apostle Paul said to Timothy…

> **2 Tim 4:3** (NIV) For the time will come when men will not put up with sound doctrine. Instead, to suit their own desires, they will gather around them a great number of teachers to say what their itching ears want to hear. 4 They will turn their ears away from the truth and turn aside to myths.

Let me close with the words of Jesus...

Luke 21:7 (NIV) "Teacher," they asked, "when will these things happen? And what will be the sign that they are about to take place?" 8 He replied: "Watch out that you are not deceived..."

Appendix

Quotes from Early Church Fathers

Justin, Dialog with Trypho, CX

"[T]wo advents of Christ have been announced: the one, in which He is set forth as suffering, inglorious, dishonored, and crucified; but the other, in which He shall come from heaven with glory, **when the man of apostasy**, who speaks strange things against the Most High, **shall venture to do unlawful deeds on the earth against us the Christians,**..." (*emphasis added*).

Constitutions of the Holy Apostles, Book VII, Sec. II, XXXII

"For in the last days false prophets shall be multiplied, and such as corrupt the word; and the sheep shall be changed into wolves, and love into hatred: for through the abounding of iniquity the love of many shall wax cold. For men shall hate, and persecute, and betray one another. **And then shall appear the deceiver of the world**, the enemy of the truth, the prince of lies, whom the Lord Jesus 'shall destroy with the spirit of His mouth, who takes away the wicked with His lips; and many shall be offended at Him. But they that endure to the end, the same shall be saved. **And then shall appear the sign of the Son of man in heaven**;' and afterwards shall be the **voice of a trumpet** by the archangel; and **in that interval shall be the revival of those that were asleep**. And then shall the Lord come, and all His saints with Him, with a great concussion above the clouds, with the angels of His power, in the throne of His kingdom, to condemn the devil, the deceiver of the world, and to render to every one according to his deeds. 'Then shall the wicked go away into everlasting punishment, but the righteous shall go into life eternal,' to inherit those things 'which eye hath not seen, nor ear heard, nor have entered into the heart of man, such things as God hath prepared for them that love Him;' and they shall rejoice in the kingdom of God, which is in Christ Jesus" (*emphasis added*).

Continue learning about the Pre-Wrath Rapture at

PrewrathMinistries.org

- Articles and websites that support Pre-Wrath
- PreWrathMinistries Newsletters
- Questions about topics or scriptures
- Communicate with Elbert Charpie
- Pre-Wrath books and resources
- Much more…

You may contact Elbert Charpie

at

elbert@prewrathministries.org

The Return

is also available in Kindle® format at Amazon.com.

Also, available in the

Google® Bookstore for Android® devices.

CPSIA information can be obtained
at www.ICGtesting.com
Printed in the USA
LVHW082148290621
691533LV00005B/447